9

POWERFUL PRACTICES

of

REALLY GREAT MENTORS

STEPHEN E. KOHN
and
VINCENT D. O'CONNELL

POWERFUL
PRACTICES

of

REALLY
GREAT
MENTORS

HOW TO INSPIRE AND
MOTIVATE ANYONE

CAREER
PRESS
Pompton Plains, N.J.

9 Powerful Practices of Really Great Mentors
Edited and Typeset by Kara Kumpel
Cover design by Rob Johnson
Printed in the U.S.A.

To order this title, please call toll-free 1-800-CAREER-1 (NJ and Cana-da: 201-848-0310) to order using VISA or MasterCard, or for further information on books from Career Press.

The Career Press, Inc.
220 West Parkway, Unit 12
Pompton Plains, NJ 07444
www.careerpress.com

Library of Congress Cataloging-in-Publication Data

CIP Data Available Upon Request.

For all the mentees with whom we have worked,
who have taught us as much as—if not more than—we have ever taught them.

Acknowledgments

Both of us have been mentored effectively, and that experience has provided us with valuable role models as well as some of the ideas presented in this book. We would like to thank the following people for their inspiring support in mentoring us in the past:

The late Dr. Paul Sherman, who provided expert guidance about how to pursue excellence as a value-adding business consultant, and Joseph Sullivan, who took a chance on a raw talent and gave the "keys to the kingdom" to someone who was still learning management and administrative skills on the job.

Contents

Foreword

by Dr. Lynn Johnson,
Dean of Business Administration,
Long Island University

My organization has a mentoring program, but the skill level of those filling the mentor role varies widely. Whereas being a mentor may be a calling, becoming a *really great* mentor actually takes a lot of practice and training. That's where the *9 Powerful Practices of Really Great Mentors* fits in. Steve Kohn and Vincent O'Connell have developed a training model that helps mentors cope with the extremely wide range of requirements for this role. After explaining the unique aspects that differentiate the mentoring role from others quite like it, Kohn and O'Connell walk readers through a series of useful mentoring practices that create an environment around the mentor–protégé relationship conducive to valuable change and enhanced new opportunities.

What I admire most about Kohn and O'Connell's approach to effectiveness in the mentoring role is the way it consistently blends together all the practices, rather than treating them as stand-alone recommendations. When discussing one practice, Kohn and O'Connell often make reference to how a previous practice augments the potency of the newly introduced distinct mentoring approach. It feels more like *9 Powerful Practices of Really Great Mentors* is really a single, albeit multidimensional approach that mentors can apply, with multiple parts that overlap considerably.

I hope you gain as much from reading this book as I did—it puts a framework around the mentoring role that is difficult to find elsewhere. It is a wonderful reference to pick up time and again, before or after meeting with a protégé. As Kohn and O'Connell write in their Introduction, if you are going to dedicate your time, resources, and personal stake in helping someone else in their career, why not gain from learning approaches that others have found most effective in guiding their protégés forward?

I wish you well in your journey to find the "inner mentor" in you. I firmly believe this book will help you do so.

Introduction

The motivation that spurs you to read a book about mentoring skills may be similar to the impetus behind your decision to become a mentor in the first place. You understand that external resources—be they books or people—can provide valuable guidance as you pursue growth opportunities. Lessons have been learned by others, and understanding that these insights exist is an integral aspect in the formation of a mentor–protégé relationship. In essence, then, you are looking for a value-adding external resource offering guidance about best practices related to developing your potential as a mentor. With this guidance, you are poised to offer more value as an external resource yourself, in supporting the learning of future protégés.

The fundamental premise underlying the effort you are making to improve your mentoring skills is sound: the better you are at the mentoring role, the more likely your protégé will benefit from the relationship. But beyond this other-oriented perspective about the value of absorbing the contents of this book, you might also be drawn in by more self-serving interests. The reciprocal learning within the mentor-protégé relationship must be very appealing to you. The outcome you seek is not simply to help protégés pursue their personal and career aspirations more effectively, but also to enable you to deem the time spent mentoring as a highly rewarding professional experience.

You may ask, *Why not just be myself and wing it?* That is, do what comes naturally while interacting with your protégé, and let the chips fall where they may. You may feel you have the hard-earned wisdom to perform as a mentor with spontaneity and an intuitive feel for what to do or say on your protégé's behalf. But for the insightful mentor, this is a myopic and undisciplined approach to performing an important professional role. The better question to ask yourself is, *If I am going to dedicate my time, resources, and personal stake in helping someone else out in his or her career, why not gain from learning approaches that others have found most effective in guiding their protégés forward?*

Because the concept of developing potential in others is so fundamental to performing in the mentor role, it is worth reflecting about in its varied contexts. Potential development is an issue with far-reaching implications across almost all dynamic societies globally. It is an issue imbued with the fundamental concept that ample rewards await individuals who possess (and wish to make full use of) various talents—education, athletics, the arts, social services, behavioral healthcare, and career development are only some of the cultural contexts within which supporting the attainment of one's full potential is central to gaining a sense of professional accomplishment, personal success, mental health, and happiness.

Certainly, here in America, developing potential is and always has been a core societal value within our culture. From our nation's Founding Fathers on through the many generations that have proceeded them right up to the present time, our society has been and continues to be based on establishing a political and social framework to maximize opportunities for those willing to reach their full potential in life. An intrinsic aspect of our national credo is that in America you can advance as far as your initiative, potential, and native talent can take you.

But Americans hardly hold a monopoly on this value set. The desire to develop one's potential is clearly embraced throughout the world, to an ever-increasing degree. Enhancing people's ability to develop their native skills and reach their potential is a moral imperative for any society that values humanity. It is what has driven recent mass uprisings in Libya, Egypt, Ukraine, and other locations around the world where many believed their government impeded rather than enhanced their desire to achieve all they can in their lives, for themselves and their children. Indeed, to *not* develop the potential within people, to deprive those with talent of the opportunity to achieve their skill-based destiny raises the idea that unfair discriminatory obstacles are in effect. Considerable social and political attention is paid—certainly here in America but increasingly throughout our Internet-connected world—to ensuring that discrimination and oppression of one's potential are eliminated or mitigated. Societies support the concept of potential-development from birth: Parents buy toys and books that initiate the process of identifying their child's special talents. We place our children in groups and instructional environments that help nurture special capabilities. Modern educational systems have been developed to uncover and unleash students' untapped potential. This has led to the creation of such innovations as Magnet Schools, competency-based tracks at every grade level, differing vocational and academic paths, and more open curricula (versus pre-arranged, universal subjects that all must study). Educational efforts are often integrated with other extramural activities, from service-oriented undertakings to sports and more, which allow students to follow a niche-based path that advances their specialized skills and interests.

To help extract the full potential of individuals and teams, we engage instructors, tutors, coaches, and others who have specialized expertise and knowledge to advance skill development and learning. Mentoring is just one of many examples of efforts organized to support talented others with specialized teaching and guidance. It is a potential-developing process that has changed history. Socrates mentored Aristotle and Plato; Jesus mentored His disciples; Josef Breuer mentored Freud, who in turn mentored Carl Jung. In current times, Warren Buffet is said to be a mentor to Bill Gates, who, through his foundation, in turn supports many educational endeavors to optimize students' potential worldwide. There are innumerable other highly notable professional mentor-protégé relationships that have created "rules-changing" innovations, technological inventions that have enhanced the lives of generations thereafter, and thought leadership that has impacted the methods used to advance to the next level in scientific, academic, organizational, and societal endeavors.

The powerful mentoring practices we share in this book are the result of contributions from those who have served as mentors, and the lessons they have learned that they have shared with us. Theories of mentoring are important to consider, but it is the practical application of successful mentoring techniques that serves as the basis for the nine powerful mentoring practices we present. For all those who discussed their impressions about mentoring with us as a way of contributing real-life experiences to the development of our 9 Powerful Practices model, we would like to express once again our sincere gratitude.

A note on terminology used in the book: you may have already noticed that we refer to recipients of a mentor's guidance as "protégés." Another term used for the protégé role is "mentee." Some mentoring theorists differentiate between the two terms depending on the framework by which the developmental, supportive, and helping activities are provided by the mentor. The "development-focused" view of mentoring typically uses the term *mentee* for the receiving end of the mentoring dyad; the "sponsorship-focused" mentoring tends to use the term *protégé*. However, we use the terms *mentee* and *protégé* rather interchangeably throughout the book, without any direct inference that the mentee or protégé is receiving a specific type of mentoring support.

We dedicate several chapters of this book to discussing organizationally-sponsored mentoring programs. These programs are valuable endeavors, in our view. However, the mentoring skills we identify are really applicable to any type of mentoring context. As our book title suggests, these skills can inspire and motivate anyone for whom you are providing individualized mentorship.

CHAPTER 1

Mentoring:
Defining a Complex, Challenging Role

"I shall not today attempt further to define the kinds of material I understand to be embraced within that shorthand description...and perhaps I could never succeed in intelligibly doing so. But I know it when I see it."

—Justice Potter Stewart, concurring opinion in Jacobellis v. Ohio 378 U.S. 184 (1964), regarding possible obscenity in *The Lovers*

As a prospective or current mentor, you are intrigued by the opportunity to perform in this professional role. Perhaps, as in most cases, you were mentored yourself, and you have experienced firsthand the value of being guided by a more senior individual in the career field you have chosen. Now that you have reached a point where you believe you have something special to offer a more junior person with professional interests similar to your own, the mentor role seems like a logical and enticing way to round out a career characterized by continuous learning and steady professional growth. It is time to "pay it forward" by providing career knowledge and guidance, and you want to do it as effectively as possible.

Once you identify that the mentor role is one you hope to play, you might ask, "How can I best help a prospective mentee? What methods should I apply to best share my background and experience, and impart the valuable wisdom I possess to the next generation?" Mentoring methods need to align with prior positive results shown through effective practice in the mentoring role. But the role is a complex one, with an unusually broad set of defining characteristics. The process of developing one's competency as a mentor involves such a broad array of sub-skills that it is truly difficult to know where to begin.

The many similar roles performed by helping and instructional professionals make it challenging to truly differentiate the essential defining characteristics of a mentor. The following list identifies 12 other support roles with striking similarities to the type of support that mentors provide.

Roles With Highly Similar Fundamental Skillsets to Mentoring

Advisor	Coach	Confidant
Counselor (e.g., school guidance)	Guru	Instructor

Manager	Master (e.g., to an apprentice)	Preceptor
Supervisor (work, clinical, etc.)	Teacher	Therapist

To mentor effectively, you will need to possess and strengthen all the fundamental skills common to these types of professionals who are in the business of providing help, guidance, and support (we discuss these skills in greater depth in the next chapter). But how do we gain an understanding of mentor-specific attributes, in order to differentiate the skills needed to be as effective as possible in this particular and unique role?

Perhaps great mentoring is the same as Justice Stewart's famous perception of obscenity, quoted at the beginning of this chapter: it is hard to define, but we know it when we see it—or experience it. Mentoring creates an emotional connection that is rather unique to the teaching, guidance, and professional support process. We have found that the true nature of mentoring is embedded within the following statement a mentee might make:

"S/he is more than a [*insert a role from the previous list*] to me—s/he is my mentor."

If this type of statement resonates with meaning to those of us who hear it, there must be a slight but distinguishable difference in the mentor role from these other helping and support roles. We need to focus on how the term *mentor* implies an expansion of the defining elements of all those previously listed helping, learning, and support roles. If our hypothetical mentee's statement has meaning, then the mentor provides a little something extra. We will try to drill into some definitions of mentoring to uncover what those "something extra" qualities really are.

Certainly, there has been no lack of attempts to clarify a common definition for the mentor role. But which definition helps uncover those "something extras"? Here are some definitions of a mentor or mentoring that we uncovered in the relevant literature:

※ Mentor (n): An experienced and trusted advisor. (Oxford English Dictionary)

※ Mentoring is offline help by one person to another in making significant transitions in knowledge, work, or thinking. (Megginson and Clutterbuck 2005)

※ A mentor is someone who helps another person to become what that person aspires to be. (Montreal CEGEP definition, cited in Kagans and Kram 2007)

※ Mentoring is a reciprocal, long-term relationship with an emotional commitment that exists between a novice (protégé) and an experienced professional (mentor); mentoring implies a knowledge or competence gradient, in which the teaching–learning process contributes to a sharing of advice or expertise, role development, and formal and informal support to influence the career of the protégé. (Mariani 2012)

※ A mentor is someone who serves variously as teacher, sponsor, advisor, and model: as teacher in enhancing the mentee's skills and intellectual development; as sponsor in using his or her influence to facilitate the protégé's entry and early advancement in the field they both inhabit; as host and guide, in helping to initiate the mentee into a new occupational and social world, acquainting him or her with its values, customs, resources, and cast of characters; as advisor, providing counsel, moral support, and direction; and through his or her own virtues, achievements, and lifestyle, serving as an exemplar whom the protégé can seek to emulate. (Wiltshire 1998)

In order to give the mentor role definition proper justice, it cannot be as simple as the Oxford Dictionary definition offers. Mentoring is certainly about advising and embodying trustworthiness, but these attributes apply to almost any helping or support role. So the dictionary definition does not really help us understand the true nature of the mentoring role.

The element of Megginson and Clutterbuck's definition of mentoring involving **"offline help"** is an apt contribution to understanding the more unique features of the mentoring role and the mentor–protégé relationship. Defining mentoring as "offline help" implies that the mentor–protégé relationship is enacted when both parties are able to convey their respective shared commitment to the mentoring process by dedicating time to it when not performing one's "day job," so to speak. Mentor–protégé interactions need extra time to provide emotional space for both parties to thoroughly process the information being discussed. Dedicated "offline" support offers opportunities to add real value within the relationship's give and take. This definition implies less direct accountability for how the process is enacted and the timing of its positive outcomes.

Mentoring, therefore, can be differentiated from a teacher who must grade the mentee/student at a set milestone every semester, an athletic coach who strives to win games or events while developing the potential of a mentee/athlete, and managers/supervisors who must rate performance and direct day-to-day work assignments of a mentee/subordinate.

Indeed, an athletic coach is not going to seek to perform in a mentoring role for a team member or an assistant coach while making judgments during the final minutes of a tie game, when the intensity of the competition captures the coach's full attention. He or she will tend to engage in mentoring opportunities on an off day, or mid-week, say, when a practice session is over. Similarly, a business-focused mentor–protégé relationship may occur after work hours or on weekends, away from the pressures and intensity of day-to-day performance deadlines and meeting customer demands.

Another aspect of the core essence of mentoring suggested by Megginson and Clutterbuck's definition is that this activity involves addressing **"significant transitions."** This implies that mentoring is characterized by the need to contemplate or work through some type of major change or movement in the mentee's life or career, such as a new job, a career advancement opportunity, or a need to cope with a major organizational change like a merger, restructuring, or downsizing. The mentor is a sounding board and advisor about how to best manage oneself amid such transitions, bolstering the protégé's adaptability to the numerous and inevitable transitions that occur throughout one's career (especially careers that involve taking on more leadership responsibility).

Consequently, when a helping- and learning-focused support role addresses issues involving taking the next career step, adding skills to achieve new or higher levels of responsibility, or exploring new professional terrain, an environment exists for mentoring to occur. This addresses the support for achievement of aspirations identified as defining mentoring by the Montreal CEGEP (Collège d'Enseignement Général et Professionnel, or College of General and Vocational Education), as it is these "next steps" to which a mentee typically aspires.

The reciprocal emotional commitment that exists between a novice and an experienced professional is another defining element of a relationship in which mentoring can be delivered. Certainly, when novices label individuals who have guided them as more than their official role (teacher, coach, advisor, and so on), but as a "mentor to me," the resonance implied in the mentee's characterization of the guidance being received contains a strong emotional component. The intensity of emotional commitment in the healthy mentor–protégé relationship is different from what one might typically have with the individual performing other types of helping or support roles. Mentoring can have an almost paternal or maternal emotional characterization, a shared emotional commitment to the mentoring relationship that leaves mentees feeling uniquely cared-for and understood. But instead of being performed in a family-based context, mentoring is delivered in the context of personal and professional development. The emotional commitment engenders gratitude from mentees for their mentor's willingness to dedicate time and commitment to their growth and future prospects within his or her chosen field, and a reciprocal paternalistic or maternalistic satisfaction from the mentor in the mentees' growth and achievement.

Mentees' emotional commitment is evident in the trust they place in their mentors and in the mentoring process, which is enhanced by the sharing that characterizes this process. It is essential that mentors recognize that they are in a trusting relationship. Their behavior must always reflect an understanding that mentoring only works when trust is evident in the mentoring process. Every powerful practice of effective mentoring we recommend has at its foundation a sincere and abiding mutual trust between protégé and mentor.

Indeed, mentoring involves building a relationship that matters a great deal to both parties. It is a relationship that engenders sincere reciprocal satisfaction when events demonstrate that the relationship is effective. Consequently, the mentor must be prepared to make an emotional commitment to the relationship being established with a mentee. By an emotional commitment, we mean a readiness to care about what is occurring in the relationship and the results achieved, and to be comfortable with having a stake in the mentee's professional growth (versus keeping one's emotional distance, as supervisors at work might do in order not to appear to have favorites among their direct reports). In short, mentoring is characterized by a willingness to make an emotional connection to the mentee, and to be committed to supporting the mentee's welfare and future.

To actualize this emotional commitment to the relationship, mentors and protégés must see the **bond as long term**. Both parties need to feel that the relationship has "legs," that it can endure despite occasional disruptions or obstacles that may emerge. For example, if one of the parties moves to a different geographic location, the relationship may turn into one that is conducted by telephone or Web tools such as Skype, but it continues. Mentoring relationships often last for a lifetime—or at least a professional lifetime. They do not have to, but the fact that they can and often do extend throughout one's career shows that it is a process that tends by definition to be longer-term. This characteristic of mentoring differentiates it from guidance focused primarily on immediate or short-term goals, which ends once those goals are met.

In her definition of mentoring, Mariani brings up the concept of the need for **guidance along a competence gradient**. Mentees seek more senior individuals for insightful teaching and advice because the profession they have chosen requires additional and more refined competencies as they works their way up the ladder to achieve success at the higher levels. Perhaps the best way to understand this defining aspect of mentoring is to consider the converse assumption: mentoring is neither required nor in demand if the mentee's learning curve is relatively flat in his or her profession, even if a "next level" within the profession might be available. The more junior individual in this circumstance may seek occasional counsel or spot advice from a more senior individual, but it would be hard to characterize this relationship as mentoring.

The competence gradient that helps define the objectives of mentoring also implies that the relationship tends to be between seasoned, experienced, senior-level individuals (who perform mentoring) and inexperienced, relatively junior-level individuals (who are their protégés). Great mentors are those who have reached a point in their career in which their competencies are higher on a profession's competence scale than others with whom they have contact. In such a circumstance, a senior professional's identity includes an implicit responsibility to develop the potential in those who demonstrate the capability to achieve the same types of goals to which they too had aspired at an earlier age. **Mentoring is an activity performed** by those who wish to make a contribution to future generations, which concomitantly helps professionals address internal altruistic needs that have often been unfulfilled at earlier stages of their careers.

In short, the best mentors are those who, because they have achieved a more senior level in their profession, embrace a responsibility to help others master what they have had to master. It is a process integral to most healthy cultures all around the world, related to elders passing on valuable knowledge to the next generation. A defining aspect of being a mentor is more than arranging to be of service to an individual with less knowledge and experience than you—it is a self-actualizing process that helps engender a sense of accomplishment and credibility as a master of one's profession.

Wiltshire's more comprehensive definition of mentoring adds the notion that **this role is multidimensional** and, by inference, adaptive to different mentee needs as they emerge. The intrinsic multidimensionality of mentoring means that performing the role requires an appreciation that any of the four primary functions—teacher, sponsor, advisor, and model— might be the most valuable to perform at any given point in the mentee's development. At one time, the mentor might be most valuable introducing the protégé to key influencers in their field, or offering the protégé an opportunity to lead a project to promote his or her professional visibility. Here, the mentor is fulfilling his or her **sponsorship** role. In another instance, the educator–pupil dyad might be the best use of the mentor and protégé's time, for example, with the mentor **teaching** about methods he or she has found effective, and the protégé acting as the attentive learner who takes mental notes to which he or she can refer back when likely to attempt the mentor's suggested method.

Mentoring is also about providing direction and serving as an **advisor** on a range of topics about which the more junior mentee seeks guidance. Actually, the term *mentor* appears first in this context: In ancient Greek mythology, the character Mentor guided and advised the young novice Telemachus at the behest of Ulysses (Odysseus), King of Ithaca. Ulysses had left his wife, Penelope, and infant son, Telemachus, in the hands of Mentor, his friend and retainer, as he went to make war on the Trojans. Mentor's role was embellished by the fact that Athena, the supreme goddess of the Greeks, took on the form of Mentor to Telemachus. Athena as Mentor appeared especially when things looked particularly bleak or confusing for Telemachus, or when critical choices had to be made. Athena embodied good counsel, prudent restraint, and practical insight. To a major degree Mentor was responsible not only for the boy's education (the teacher role), but for the shaping of his character, the wisdom of his decisions, and the clarity and steadfastness of his purpose (the advisor role).

Mentors are also defined by the value they offer in **modeling desirable behaviors**. The learning of specialized skills is not as simple as hearing how to do something, or listening to sage advice. Mentees' learning is enhanced when they can see prudent, productive, effective, and results-generating behaviors in action. Seeing is believing, as the saying goes. Modeling the effective behaviors discussed between mentor and protégé reinforces their validity. This is why a mentor might invite a protégé to attend one of his or her presentations to demonstrate platform-speaking techniques. It is why a mentor might suggest that the protégé participate on a team the mentor leads (or performs a prominent role in) pertinent to the protégé's future aspirations. Modeling allows the mentee to observe behaviors worth emulating. This includes behaviors that the mentor demonstrates in the direct interactions that occur throughout the mentor–protégé relationship, such as empathic listening and seeking first to understand before trying to be understood. We will discuss more about modeling behaviors later, in Chapter 6.

The complexity of performing in the mentor role lies in the challenge one experiences selecting the best choice among the four primary mentor roles to apply when addressing one of the mentee's needs. Mentoring requires a range of basic skills, but choosing the best mentor role to promote the mentee's learning and development is a highly intuitive process, more art than science. It takes practice (trying different tactics among these defining roles of the mentor) and then observing results. When the role you choose hits the target and promotes your protégé's development, the mentoring process is immensely satisfying. It is what makes performing in this role so intrinsically interesting, dynamic, and rewarding.

———

The composite definition of mentoring, therefore, offers important understandings about the "something extra" that embodies the true nature of the role as compared to a range of similar helping, instructional, and interpersonal support roles. You may wonder, *None of these defining elements of mentoring are truly exclusive to the role: therapists provide offline help; guidance counselors at school address an individual student's aspirations; many coaches make an emotional commitment to their athletes or teams. How are these definitions unique to mentoring?* It is true, each defining element is far from being exclusive to mentoring. But mentoring involves the unique blending of *all* of these defining elements into a single support role.

Perhaps the "something extra" in the mentor role we are trying to define is just this: manifesting the judgment, wisdom, and emotional commitment to apply the right offline learning, advice, sponsoring opportunities, and role-modeling behaviors to more junior individuals who seek such support within a trusting relationship. Effective mentors show understanding and competencies for all specific traits that define their role, but they also know how and when to demonstrate these skills in response to the protégé's unique learning needs. And when these choices are on target, mentees feel an enhanced emotional connection to the learning process and to the mentor him- or herself.

Summary

The aspects which, together as a group, help define the unique nature of serving as a mentor include:

※ **Being ready to provide help "offline."** The mentor–protégé relationship is best conceptualized as career training and professional development that occurs separately from the performance of immediate duties, or from accountability for a certain immediate result. It requires time and emotional space to enable reflection about the value and meaning of certain behaviors. With respect to the sponsor role of a mentor, efforts to introduce a protégé to the people and processes of a special professional group or expand the protégé's contacts within relevant spheres of influence can be useful offline activities for the mentor to initiate. Consequently, a mentor must be prepared to commit to a meaningful relationship with a mentee that will require extra effort and time beyond the performance of one's own professional responsibilities.

✳ **Understanding that mentoring is about preparing your mentee for the next step(s), as opposed to where he or she is now.** Mentors prepare mentees for significant transitions in knowledge, work, and thinking. Often, these transitions are those to which mentees aspire. The characteristic seniority of mentors enables them to add particular value and perspective about proceeding to the next logical step in one's career, with a greater understanding of the forward step's challenges and required additional competencies.

✳ **Guiding your mentee up the learning curve.** Mentoring is defined by support that accelerates the process of gaining applicable professional competencies. The steeper the learning curve, the more a mentor is capable of adding value. Mentoring offers ongoing opportunities to engender lasting value in supporting mentees' efforts to achieve milestones along a professional learning path.

✳ **Embracing mentoring as a relationship, with a future**. This is because mentoring involves a reciprocal emotional commitment, over the long term. Mentoring is not an activity characterized by maintaining rigid professional boundaries or emotional distancing, undertaken with a short "window of opportunity" timeframe. When mentoring is performed effectively, mentees feel cared for, uniquely understood, and part of a trust-filled relationship that typically endures beyond the occurrence of temporary or unforeseen obstacles or interruptions. Mentors care about their protégés' immediate and longer-term future. There is an emotional resonance between protégé and mentor when the relationship is an effective and potent one, which often lasts a professional lifetime.

✳ **Wearing many mentoring hats.** The mentoring role is multidimensional, adapting teaching, advising, sponsoring and modeling to the mentee's specific needs.

———

The 9 Powerful Practices of Really Great Mentors that we share in this book can be traced back to one or more activities that define the mentor role. But first, we should revisit the core skills that serve as the underlying foundation for how these 9 Powerful Practices add potency to the mentoring process.

CHAPTER 2

Fundamentals of Effective Mentoring

Personal trainers and yoga instructors often focus on the "core" as they start developing their clients' or students' strength, flexibility, endurance, and health. In this chapter, we will share this emphasis on the core, but in our case, we change the context from physical fitness to interpersonal understandings and competencies needed to most effectively implement the 9 Powerful Practices of Really Great Mentors model. In essence, we are providing you the same type of advice you might use in certain circumstances with a future protégé: "Let's take first things first." Before we begin describing a useful set of proven practices to advance your capabilities as a mentor, let's begin by reviewing some basic fundamentals that will make our proposed model as impactful as possible.

In the previous chapter we attempted to differentiate aspects of mentoring from other forms of personal or professional guidance, and in this chapter we take the opposite tack: Here, we want to underscore that when you choose to become a support-providing helper to another person—as a mentor is—you will need to develop and apply skills that are so common to effective teachers, advisors, or those who guide others professionally that these skills are almost like second nature. Whether you are a coach to a player, therapist to a client/patient, manager to a direct report, trade master to an apprentice, or in a mentoring role to a protégé, you will perform your role with more success if you demonstrate a set of "people" or "soft" skills that typify those with the capability to nurture an other-oriented, growth-focused relationship.

Many of the core attributes of an effective mentor are captured in the concepts that define one's emotional intelligence. Whereas the best mentors tend to be smart about the more technical elements and nuances of whatever it is that they do for a living, they also must show a different kind of intelligence: They need to be smart about what motivates others in a forward-aiming direction. They must have emotional radar that senses what their protégé is feeling, and what they too are feeling during the guidance process. To be an effective mentor, your EQ (level of emotional intelligence) needs to be at least as high as—if not higher than—your IQ (more academic or conceptual understanding–based smarts).

A wide range of research and literature exists about what motivates individuals to improve, learn more, and achieve more, and how to facilitate this process as an external resource. This is the fundamental context in which mentoring takes place. Certainly, a review of all this literature is well beyond the scope of this book. Much of it, in fact, is of very little assistance to someone interested in developing skills as a mentor. But we have chosen three principles of facilitating self-learning that are fundamental to implementing the helping role effectively:

1. Self-actualization
2. Self-awareness-building
3. Becoming more naturally empathic

1. Self-Actualization

Many of you may have studied behavioral sciences during your formal education, and if you did it is almost certain that you were exposed to the work of Abraham Maslow, who introduced a "Hierarchy of Needs" theory in the mid-20th century that still resonates today. Maslow's Hierarchy of Needs has helped reframe approaches to the management role, steering leaders away from financially or threats-based motivational frameworks of leadership and toward a model that assumes that people work in order to gain personal fulfillment. Maslow's model postulated that what people really want out of life, once they are not in a varying degree of "pure survival mode," is self-actualization; that is, incremental growth toward attainment of the individual's highest needs—those related to the meaning in life, in particular.

The context of self-actualization in mentoring rarely takes on the overarching topic of the meaning of life; more often, mentoring addresses the real-life issues of fulfillment in one's work life, such as, "What is the meaning of what I do professionally?" Or "What impacts does my work have, on both those around me and the environment in which I practice, and how can I make these impacts better for all concerned?" or "What outcomes would make me feel most fulfilled in my work life?" In addressing these questions, the mentor and protégé discuss issues with a profound bearing on the focus of the protégé's future efforts, driven by an understanding of what the protégé's real objectives are in actualizing a meaningful professional career.

2. Self-Awareness-Building

A leading management coach, John Whitmore, wrote that "what I am aware of empowers me, and what I am unaware of controls me." For mentors, this statement has profound meaning in a wide variety of ways. When the mentor-protégé relationship uncovers a more evidence-based understanding of the protégé's strengths and weaknesses, development plans can be devised to leverage protégés' strengths and mitigate the impact of their weaknesses—or somehow find a way to improve on the weaknesses until they are not considered weaknesses any longer. But it takes courage and emotional will to explore one's strengths and challenges. Mentors must engender an ongoing and open exploration of the protégé's self-awareness, within the context that Whitmore advocates: personal and professional empowerment through increased self-knowledge, and the uncovering of blind spots that can diminish professional effectiveness.

Emotional self-awareness is of particular importance. Mentors need to be aware of their protégés' and their own emotional "temperature" during mentoring interactions and throughout the tenure of the relationship. Emotional self-awareness is, in essence, knowing what you are feeling and why, as well as what others appear to be feeling, and why. If, for example, a mentor is aware of a feeling of personal frustration about an issue or interaction with a mentee, it is important to at least understand that emotion and why the feeling is evident at that particular point in time. What you do about this understanding can vary, from sharing it with the protégé (rarely a bad idea, since it is part of the reality of the moment, and enhances mutual awareness within the relationship) to causing additional discussions of alternatives because the one being enacted is creating frustration.

Similarly, effective mentors gauge emotional reactions from protégés to certain stimuli, such as a prodding question or discussion of a prior troublesome event. Mentors need to be comfortable reflecting the feelings of their protégés and owning up to their own while mentoring is underway.

3. Becoming More Naturally Empathic

One of Steven Covey's "7 Habits of Highly Effective People" is "Seek first to understand, then to be understood." This advice needs to become the mentor's mantra. The mentor role is typified by significant efforts to understand the protégé as a person and a professional far before lending any guidance or advice. Mentoring without seeking first to understand is not mentoring at all; it is facile advice-giving without context.

One mentor we know keeps Covey's "seek first to understand, then to be understood" habit of highly successful people as a placard on his desk, so that when protégés are prone to ask, "So what do you think I should do?" he is able to point to the placard and reply, "I don't think I know enough about what is going on yet. Let's try to understand it all better." Then he asks an open-ended probing question to elicit more information. This is the type of basic empathic behavior that facilitates mentoring, and yields more success in the relationship with a protégé.

Indeed, seeking first to understand before needing to be understood is a proxy for developing the skill of empathy. In *9 Powerful Practices of Really Great Bosses*, a book we recently wrote to improve the people skills of managers, we defined *empathy* as "the capacity to understand and respond effectively to the unique experience of another." Sounds applicable to the mentoring role, doesn't it? But how does one become more naturally empathic, in order to build a base from which they can serve more effectively in the role of helper?

The following techniques all apply to those seeking to become useful to a protégé while serving in the role of mentor:

⁂ **Ask open-ended questions.** By applying techniques of effective listening, mentors can transform the communication with their mentee into a joint exploration of the issue at hand. Use bridging statements to elicit information, rather than questions that can be answered with a yes or no. By "bridging statements," we mean starting an examination of an issue with a statement rather than a question; for example, start with "So, tell me more about...," or rephrase the mentee's words by saying, "So, what I am hearing from you is that...[re-phrase what you heard]. Tell me more about why that was important to you." The opposite approach—asking simply, "Would you agree that [state your interpretation of an event]?"—establishes a framework that can minimize rather than enhance understanding. A complementary aspect of this technique is to substitute statements for closed-ended questions that begin with the word *Why*. Using an opening that elicits information, such as, "Tell me more about the reasons that led you to that decision," offers far better opportunities for mutual understandings than the more direct and potentially defensiveness-engendering question, "Why did you do that?" Your interpersonal communication techniques need to be focused on *adding to understanding*. Questions that begin with *Why* tend to engender emotionally defensive reactions, which decrease rather than increase the opportunities you have to attain additional relevant information.

※ **Slow down.** Empathy is a skill that is best expressed at a slower pace. Remember how we defined mentoring in part as "offline help"? The offline nature of mentoring is important because it enables the mentor and protégé to slow down and explore issues at a pace not impacted by immediate professional or personal demands. If you find yourself hurried when performing in a mentoring role, you are probably reflecting a lack of willingness to understand and respond to the protégé's unique circumstances. And he or she will feel this behavior as emotional distancing. Often, the result is the mentee feeling far less trust in and appreciation for the mentoring process.

※ **Let the story unfold.** Empathy, like mentoring, is by nature almost the opposite of the "quick fix."

41

Mentors may perceive errors in judgment or in actions by their protégé almost immediately upon hearing the circumstances under discussion. Your knee-jerk reaction may be to stop the protégé almost immediately and share your view about how the issue could have been handled more effectively, from your perspective of possessing greater experience and seasoned wisdom about such matters. But mentors need to a) be aware of this need or compulsion to provide the quick fix that solves the problem easily and expediently, and b) temper this need or compulsion to dole out advice reactively, by applying techniques that enable the protégé's story to unfold at a deeper and more thoughtful level. When tempted to dole out a quick fix, apply empathic bridging techniques instead: "Let's explore what happened more—I think doing that is important. Tell me some of the things that were on your mind and what you were feeling as this incident occurred."

✳ **Set limits when the protégé demonstrates avoidant or "let's change the topic" behaviors.** The mentor–protégé relationship occurs in a context of personal change and growth, and as the saying goes, "no pain, no gain." When the discussion focuses on changing the way the mentee responds to circumstances or the mentor attempts to reframe certain events in a way that is likely to cause at least some emotional discomfort in the mentee, resistant behaviors may emerge. The mentee may attempt to subtly swerve the discussion off topic, remain silent, or seek out environmental stimuli to change the discussion away from the issue ("Excuse me, I think I just received a text message that I need to respond to," or "I really like that print you have on your wall; who is the artist?"). In these circumstances, empathic mentors understand the discomfort their protégés are feeling, and interpret the deflections or topic-changing behaviors as natural but avoidant responses to such discomfort. Reflecting the feeling is a useful limit-setting measure that mentors can apply to continue a painful discussion: "It seems as if you are trying to change the topic, which might mean you are not comfortable working through what we are discussing. Tell me more about why that is, from your perspective."

✳ **Become an avid listener.** The famous 80/20 Pareto Principle can be applied to efforts focused on seeking first to understand. To be an effective mentor, one should be listening 80 percent of the time and speaking 20 percent of the time, on average. Listening is a skill that can be developed with discipline and focus, even if you feel it does not come naturally to you. How do you know if listening is not a natural skill for you? Here is a list of ineffective listening behaviors against which you can make a self-assessment:

✳ While the other person is speaking, do you spend mental time rehearsing what you are going to say once they stop, or once they give you any opportunity to interrupt?

※ Do you pick up on certain phrases or pieces of the speaker's statements, and largely ignore the rest?

※ Do you make up your mind about the person's circumstances without hearing the entire scope or context of what you are being told?

※ Do you tend to immediately connect everything you hear to yourself, instead of considering and focusing on the other person's unique circumstances?

※ Do you filter what people say through the lens of personal biases and prejudices that you hold about people and behaviors, which you consider immutable truths?

※ Do you hear and only respond to the content being shared, and never to what you believe is being left unspoken, especially about the dynamics or emotions that exist between you and the speaker?

※ The discipline and focus needed to become an avid listener are best implemented through a range of techniques: attending, acknowledging, and supporting; restating and paraphrasing content; reflecting feelings; summarizing, interpreting, and synthesizing; and probing.

※ *Attending, acknowledging, and supporting:* Providing verbal or nonverbal awareness of, and support to, the protégé—for example, eye contact, nodding one's head, and smiling. Effective mentors are attentive during discussions with their protégés, and show listening behaviors that support idea-sharing and demonstrate that attention is being paid.

✳ *Restating and paraphrasing content:* Mimicking or rephrasing the protégé's words and asking for more information about what prompted the protégé to make the statement he or she did is an effective listening technique.

✳ *Reflecting feelings:* Mentors need to be comfortable probing into emotional content by replying with responses that prompt their protégé to enhance his or her emotional self-awareness. A good way to perform this effective listening behavior is to reply, "It sounds like you felt [state the feeling you perceive] during that situation," or, "That must have been frustrating for you." Then wait for a response to this cue to explore feelings in the circumstances being discussed.

✳ *Summarizing, interpreting, and synthesizing:* These are techniques that offer a tentative interpretation of the protégé's feelings, desires, or meanings, to elicit the protégé's response to such interpretations. Avid listeners do not automatically assume these interpretations are valid just because they voiced them. But through efforts to understand how "putting A and B together might mean C," you take the listening to a new and higher plane that enhances your shared understanding about what is occurring.

✳ *Probing:* Asking additional questions that pertain to the issues being discussed is valuable during mentoring interactions. The more pertinent the probing question, the more impactful this listening technique is. A common probing question in a mentor–protégé relationship is, "How do you believe your decision/statement/e-mail/report was perceived by others or those who received it? How do you know about this reaction to your work?" Probing offers opportunities for important data to emerge that can inform future discussions.

Summary

A set of three core skills—supporting self-actualization, self-awareness-building, and becoming more naturally empathic—serve as the underlying basis for implementing the nine mentoring techniques we will discuss later in the book. Without integrating, developing, and applying these skills to our model, you will not be able to achieve the level of success you no doubt were hoping to realize when you decided to learn more about effective mentoring techniques. To re-emphasize the important themes we have raised in this chapter, we advocate that:

✳ **Mentoring is really about self-actualization**, the apex of Maslow's Hierarchy of Needs: exploring what fulfills your protégé professionally and personally makes mentoring the most effective.

✕ **It's not about you.** Mentors seek first to understand, not to be understood. They practice empathy. Mentoring is an other-oriented activity; consequently, mentors need to refine their skills focused on letting the story unfold and responding to the unique circumstances of protégés.

✕ **If it's not about you, then you'll have to be an avid and effective listener.** The art of listening to understand is critical to mentoring success. At the very least, do your best to follow the 80/20 rule of time spent listening versus time spent speaking, to establish the environment in which seeking first to understand can occur.

CHAPTER 3

Mentoring at Work:
Advantages and Challenges

Organizations recognize that mentoring offers opportunities to achieve a competitive advantage in their industry. If they are able to use mentoring programs to optimize their internal talent, the results can be exceptional. Conversely, they understand that neglecting the potential within their organizations raises substantial and meaningful opportunity costs, such as:

※ **People improvement–related opportunity costs**: Why search elsewhere for talent to fill open positions when current staff can be groomed for them? Searching elsewhere for talent incurs expenses that might be avoided if the organization can promote from within. And how do talented people feel when they witness open positions being filled by outsiders, when these positions would be part of a logical career development plan for them? They may leave, which incurs additional costs for the organization to replace them. If people are the organization's most valuable asset, then developing their full potential is how the organization can optimize these assets.

✳ **Process improvement–related opportunity costs:** Talented people innovate, and they think about process improvements innovatively. Conversely, talented people who feel stuck in a rigid environment that is resistant to change will leave the organization or lose motivation to apply their innovative skills. By using mentoring to support efforts to channel talent toward discovering better ways to deliver solutions, organizations can streamline their business processes, accelerate the delivery of products and services to customers, improve quality, and capitalize on creating a culture of innovation.

✳ **Technology improvement–related opportunity costs:** Talented people are creative, and they're driven to create the proverbial "better mouse trap." These days, the better mouse trap is often associated with developing new technological advances. Are there individuals in your firm who could create the next major advance in applied technology? In our digital, Internet-mediated world, the drive to experiment and create new and better ways of doing things or to engage technology users in a more interactive way is now a societal norm.

Perhaps some new solution is lying dormant in the brains of someone working in your organization today. Your organization would be wise not to lose the opportunity to unleash this potential.

The following chart conveys the results of matching organizationally sponsored talent-enhancing resources (such as coaching, mentoring, and focused career training) with different levels of role-congruent potential (in other words, talents that could be leveraged by the organization if they were developed to their fullest).

HIGH	**❸** WASTED POTENTIAL: CONSIDERABLE UNTAPPED POTENTIAL WITHIN ORGANIZATION	**❹** LEVERAGING PEOPLE'S TALENT: WITH RESULTING INCREASED PRODUCTIVITY, LOYALTY, SUCCESS
LOW	**❶** TALENT STASIS: LITTLE OPPORTUNITY FOR PEOPLE TO DRIVE VALUE WITHIN ORGANIZATION	**❷** WASTED RESOURCES: POTENTIAL- DEVELOPMENT ACTIVITIES CREATE LITTLE ADDED VALUE

Role-Congruent Potential in Organization

LOW — Time/Resources Dedicated to Potential-Development — HIGH

This chart raises a number of fundamental questions related to potential development within the organization:

1. Which individuals in your organization may be ripe for targeted potential-development activities and strategies?

2. How much role-congruent potential exists within the individuals at your company who hold positions with significant advancement opportunities?

3. What is the correct amount of time, and what are the correct types of potential development resources to be dedicated to those individuals?

4. How does the organization measure the results of a dedicated potential-development effort or strategy?

5. If mentoring those with high potential is likely to add significant value, what methods of developing potential have proven most effective?

The first four fundamental questions, which involve human-resources-management strategies to assess ways to optimize and manage the talent in your organization, are not what this book seeks to address. What we hope to accomplish in this book is to answer question #5—to raise the level of competency in performing as a value-adding mentor to those with significant upside potential. In truth, our belief is that the effectiveness of addressing the issues raised by questions 1 through 4 will be less salient if the individuals performing the potential-development activity of mentoring talented people *do not have the skills or sound fundamental approaches to deliver* on a mentoring program's promise of unleashing vast, value-adding potential.

Nonetheless, it is useful to consider the causes of the four outcomes shown in Figure 1. The outcome shown in quadrant ❶, Talent Stasis, may arise out one of the following factors:

1. The organization has repetitive, more mechanical tasks, and places a higher premium on matching here-and-now skills in performing and/or leading these tasks rather than developing future skills (because the work will not change much).

2. There is a poor selection of people in positions the organization would like to support with development efforts, thus creating a sense that an investment in potential development is largely a fruitless endeavor.

In an environment of Talent Stasis, the blind spot for the organization might be in failing to see that supervisory personnel of valuable yet repetitive functions wish to grow professionally, and that the organization risks losing the person to another organization or losing an opportunity to engender more loyalty from him or her to the enterprise. Another possible blind spot might be in holding on to a myopic view of the future, choosing to ignore the reality that change, and the evolution of the enterprise over time, is inevitable.

In quadrant ❷, Wasted Resources, the organization applies resources to developing the potential of those without a big "upside" along the competence gradient. This quadrant speaks to the issue of *selecting the right people* to involve in mentoring processes. A broad-based mentoring program of all employees from the lowest to the highest pay grade may show equity, but it also may waste valuable time and resources.

The outcome in quadrant ❸, Wasted Potential, occurs when vast talent exists in the organization's more junior levels, but it is untapped. In this scenario, the organization under-appreciates the talent assets it possesses within its human capital, and holds a myopic view of whether organizational resources are best spent in trying to maximize people's potential. As noted already, there are opportunity costs associated with maintaining such a viewpoint. It is likely that talented individuals who perceive a lack of support related to building their skills and fostering their career growth may end up leaving for other, more attractive opportunities to spread their wings and fully realize their potential.

This book is intended to help individual managers and their organizations achieve better results by combining the high potential of the people they lead with the efficient use of mentors' time, resources, and skills. In quadrant ❹, Leveraging People's Talent, the right protégés receive *the right amount of time and resources* to develop their potential, *from the right mentors*. This outcome is the holy grail of organizational mentoring systems.

Workplace-based or career-focused mentoring is an extension of the long, successful history of supporting talent through individualized professional guidance. Organizations know full well that many of the breakthrough success stories in history can be traced to protégés absorbing the guidance of a well-matched mentor. The fact that mentoring is far more institutionalized now than ever before demonstrates that organizations and businesses recognize the potential return on investment offered by formally sponsored mentoring programs at work.

The following are five prominent reasons organizations in search of an environment that achieves the desired results (quadrant ❹, Leveraging People's Talent) are likely to put forth when establishing and sponsoring an institutional mentoring program. The reasons overlap extensively; thus, the rationale for mentoring systems involves both the collection of and the interplay between multiple mutually dependent factors.

1. **To develop potential more effectively, and to support professional development functions within an organization.** Creating and administering a mentoring system improves your organization's ability to uncover and unleash talent, with its logical accompanying benefits of identifying those ripe for increased levels of responsibility and success. By pairing junior-level staff with more senior-level staff, a mentoring system creates an environment in which talent can be nurtured and executive skills modeled for those upon whom the organization will need to rely as future opportunities arise. For enterprises in a growth mode, mentoring can facilitate the ability to place well-groomed talent within newly developed departments or divisions, new field offices, or new subsidiary companies.

   Most organizations have methods to assess employees' performance and their potential to assume roles of increased responsibility. Mentoring programs provide a means to integrate individualized career support into professional development planning systems for organizations serious about enhancing their talent management capabilities.

2. **To improve staff retention and loyalty.** The feeling of being cared for that comes from the emotional commitment of a mentor–protégé relationship can engender a parallel emotional commitment to the entity sponsoring the creation and continuation of that relationship. Workplace research investigations into the variables that most positively impact the retention of desired staff reveal that gratitude for the employing organization's efforts to develop one's skills and professional development is very high on lists of reasons why individuals remain loyal to and continue working for an organization. Protégés tend to be very loyal to their mentors and often view growth within the firm where the mentor works as their best professional alternative.

Research has explored the connection between mentoring and a concept referred to as Affective Organizational Commitment, or AOC. Mentoring can be used by organizations as a means to create positive "affective events" at work—a fancy way of saying that when individuals have fulfilling emotional reactions to the circumstances they find themselves in at work, they tend to want to stay within such an emotionally reinforcing environment. Mentoring of the type we describe in this book targets this phenomenon: mentors can assist their protégés to process emotional reactions to workplace experiences, which can positively influence their emotional connection to their organization.

3. **To induct new staff into organizational norms more quickly and effectively.** Some organizations assign a mentor to new hires during the onboarding process to facilitate a supportive relationship with a more senior professional from day one of the new hire's employment. While such systems may not in fact be mentoring as we define it, the learning that emerges from this type of orientation can be quite valuable for an organization with a certain corporate culture and unique or specialized behavioral norms. Such mentoring programs pair a new employee with someone with the experience and knowledge to be a resource during the often stressful "ramp-up" process intrinsic to beginning a new job within these organizations.

4. **To support organizational change and coping with transitions.** Because mentoring by definition is a process that focuses on working through professional transitions, organizations experiencing substantial change can benefit from systemic mentoring programs that help support the success of these changes. Personnel management and leadership practice are put under considerable pressure during periods of organizational change. Mentoring programs offer the opportunity to mitigate some of the risks associated with talent drains as the organizations works through its significant transitions.

5. **To encourage and support those who might be at some sort of disadvantage within the organizational or professional environment.** Certainly, women come to mind in this regard, although

breaking through the glass ceiling at many corporations is not just occurring but becoming the norm. When true disadvantages to realizing one's potential are evident, though, mentoring opportunities provided by those who have coped with and overcome such obstacles can be very useful.

Summary

Organizations that establish or seek to establish formal mentoring programs need to consider their fundamental objectives in doing so. The basic question that helps frame efforts to develop a more formally sponsored mentoring program within an organization is this:

How do we best leverage available domain, institutional, and professional core competencies to develop future potential in the many who would benefit from being exposed to this expertise, within a mentoring-based system?

Certainly, this is a good question to ask—and one that companies continue to struggle with answering. The holy grail of organizationally sponsored mentoring is **leveraging people's talent** by using the experience and skills of more senior professionals to guide those with considerable future potential. It is quite simple to establish mentoring systems that help indoctrinate new employees to a job's requirements and a company's norms; it is *de rigeur* to establish a preceptor program for certain professionals entering the field, such as nurses. But how does the organization set up a framework that yields the types of talent-leveraging advances that have characterized highly effective mentoring through history? We explore this issue in the following chapter.

CHAPTER 4

———

Effective Matching of Mentor and Protégé

Despite all the strategic interest organizations have in mentoring, matches made between mentors and protégés often develop quite naturally and without any official or organizational sponsorship. Informal mentoring relationships develop when the need to optimize a protégé's potential is evident, as observed concurrently by a prospective mentor and by the individual this mentor knows who performs at a more junior level.

The matching process may be born out of the impression a prospective mentor such as yourself has that the protégé is struggling with the same types of issues you had to face earlier in your career, and how advisory assistance from more senior professionals was valuable to you in addressing these challenges. Mentors in effective mentor–protégé relationships often see a lot of themselves in their protégé. Similarly, protégés will tend to approach mentors for learning and support when they view these individuals as skilled role models for the types of positions to which the protégés aspire. Protégés want what their mentors have, and are eager to absorb the knowledge and skills mentors have gained through the years. Mentoring provides a means of extracting the wisdom you possess to support advancement in your protégé's personal and professional life.

When this circumstance occurs—when mentor and protégé mutually identify the protégé's needs and then begin a learning process to support these needs—the match is deemed "informal," to differentiate it from organizationally created matches, which we refer to as "formal mentoring." Participants in such informally developed mentor–protégé relationships report that mutual attraction or chemistry sparked their development. When informal mentor–protégé matches occur, it is more likely that the result will be the type of emotional resonance we have identified as critical to effective mentoring.

Mentoring may begin after the mentor has been providing other types of support in a teaching or helping role, but then it blossoms into the type of special connection that typifies a resonant mentor–protégé relationship. Perhaps your interest in the subject of effective mentoring comes from the informal mentor–protégé relationship that has already developed between you and a more junior professional. Now you are seeking guidance about how to best fill this role. Be encouraged by the fact that you already have an advantage—there is a strong likelihood that such a naturally developed relationship will be satisfying both to your protégé and to you.

Informal matching is the best way for a mentor–protégé relationship to begin—it was certainly how all of the famous mentor–protégé relationships began: Freud was not *directed* to mentor Jung; the relationship evolved out of common interests and Jung's impression that Freud was a worthy role model to emulate and learn from. Consequently, if a natural, informal mentor–protégé relationship develops between you and a more junior individual, you have accelerated the process of creating value out of the relationship. You have been able to bypass the stage that a formally established mentor–protégé match must work through: getting the mentor and protégé to know and trust each other, finding the areas of mutual interest, and uncovering how the mentoring process can add value for the protégé.

Formal mentoring, by way of contrast, facilitates the matching of mentor and protégé under the auspices of an organizationally sponsored mentoring program. Organizations understand the value in facilitating the mentoring of their competent and aspiring junior professionals, and advocate that a formal mentoring program, although never likely to achieve the consistently positive outcomes of informal mentoring, is better than having no mentoring occur at all. The notion behind the strategy to effect more mentoring within one's organization is often to simulate (or perhaps the better word is *stimulate*) the process of informally developed matches between mentor and protégé.

According to Tammy Allen, a professor of psychology at the University of South Florida and coauthor of *Designing Workplace Mentoring Programs: An Evidence-Based Approach*, "As a researcher, I can tell you that how you best match people is probably the issue where we know the least." The process most often used simulates a dating service, with the protégés in control of the selection of the mentor with whom they would like to try to create a meaningful mentoring relationship. Allowing protégés to have substantial input into their match with a mentor seems to be the most successful way of creating mentoring relationships when no prior relationship exists.

As a prospective mentor, you can raise your hand and indicate to your organization a willingness to mentor others, and then let the organization find someone for you to mentor. Organizations may ask their more senior-level professionals to join a panel of prospective mentors, but selection of a mentor is in the protégé's control. Prospective protégés can then choose their desired mentor based on similarity of career path, even if these prospective protégés do not know you personally or professionally.

One way to enable mentor–protégé matching is to have mentors fill out a "mentor profile" about their background and what they hope to offer or obtain from a mentoring relationship. The underlying concept is to match protégé and mentor based on whom they are each most likely to get along with. Dr. Liz Selzer, a consultant with a California-based consultancy called The Mentoring Group, which oversees leadership development for more than 30,000 leaders in the nonprofit sector, suggests such a method to reinforce the likelihood of rapid bonding between protégé and mentor. "If people get along," she notes, "they'll stay in the pair longer." ("How to Start a Mentoring Program"; Inc. emagazine, *www.inc.com/guides/2010/04/start-mentoring-program.html*)

Similar to information provided in an online dating service, the Mentor Profile provides prospective protégés with information they might perceive as most relevant to their selection of a mentor with whom they might be able to form a rapid bond, and whose background and experience aligns with identified development needs. The profile is intended to facilitate a down-selection process by the protégé, which may result in prearranged mutual interviews between a protégé and a short list of prospective mentors who meet the protégé's criteria.

The Mentor Profile needs to provide the right information to the mentee, to support sound matching of protégé and mentor. We would recommend grouping the Mentor Profile into four distinct categories:

1. Demographic/Background
2. Professional Career Path
3. Special Professional Interests
4. Personal Interests

1. Demographic/Background Information

The following bullet points describe some significant demographic and background data that can be valuable for prospective mentors to share, to facilitate productive mentor–protégé matching.

※ **Age.** Some protégés will seek very senior professionals, to take advantage of the experience they inevitably bring, whereas others may want a mentor a bit closer to them in age, fearing that a generation gap may hinder the rapport they hope to develop with their mentor

※ **Place of Residence.** Protégés may be attracted to a mentor from the same city where they live, or from a known location to which they have some common connection. Obviously, being from the same city enables opportunities for mentoring contacts and socialization, but knowing where the mentor lives also can give the protégé a sense of who the mentor is and his or her values. For example, if a mentor lives in a very rural area, it reflects an appreciation for a particular way of life, fostered away from cities and more intensely populated areas—much different from the lifestyle of a mentor whose city residence reflects that he or she is more likely to be an "urban animal."

✳ **Academic Background.** Knowing where a mentor studied in high school, as an undergraduate, and, if applicable, at a graduate level can create instant rapport when a protégé is also an alumnus of the same school or has some powerful ties to the institution (for example, his or her mother or father went to the school, or taught there, or it is in the same league as the school the protégé attended). Academic affiliation can be a powerful influence on building a bond between protégé and mentor, especially because younger protégés may remain quite connected to their undergraduate or graduate schools and consider their identity as highly integrated with being an alumnus of the school. The potential exists to reflect back together about the value of the academic and extracurricular experience at the school, the relationships built there that they may have in common, and even the rooting interest they may share in the school's intercollegiate sporting teams.

A significant difference in academic background may hinder the pairing of protégé and mentor, especially if the pair studied very different subjects and have little in common academically.

✳ **Marital and Family Status.** Protégés may be at a point in their lives when work-life balance is a prevalent issue and child-rearing is a significant part of their sense of self-actualization. Their personal identity may be highly aligned to their role as a parent. Protégés that are parents will invariably speak about their marriage and children, and they may hope that their mentor brings valuable perspectives and wisdom to this aspect of life, in addition to offering professionally oriented insights.

✳ **Ethnicity.** Whereas sharing one's ethnic background on paperwork raises the specter of biases or prejudices among protégés when selecting a mentor, there are many benefits to providing this information. Protégés may sense a higher likelihood of success in building rapport with someone who shares their ethnic or religious background. In systems that put protégés in control of the selection process, it is limiting to exclude such information. In the end, the choice about whether to use this information about ethnicity or to ignore it is up to the protégé. This section of a Mentor Profile is often cited as optional information. It is up to the mentor whether they wish to provide it.

2. Professional Career Path Data

* **Current Job, Title, Roles, and Responsibilities.** Protégés will want to know a lot about a prospective mentor's current job and duties. By extension, protégés will also want to understand the authority the position has to make significant decisions within the organization, what types of decisions the mentor actually makes, the level of seniority the prospective mentor has achieved within the corporate hierarchy, and to what position the mentor reports directly.

   Mentoring is often highly effective when the prospective mentor's position is one that the mentor may aspire to, even if such an aspiration is a stretch goal. But the mentor's title may not reveal his or her actual day-to-day responsibilities, so it is important for the prospective mentor to be rather detailed about what he or she does on a routine basis. For example, if the mentoring is likely to involve skill development in managing people, it is important that the protégé know how many and which positions report to the prospective mentor currently. This information provides the basis for assessing whether the prospective mentor's current relevant experience provides a strong match with the protégé's self-identified learning needs.

* **Previous Positions and Employers.** While a prospective mentor need not necessarily have experienced the exact career path that the protégé hopes

to follow, it is valuable for the protégé to assess whether a prospective mentor has faced the types of challenges the protégé currently faces or is likely to face in order to achieve his or her professional goals. It is valuable for protégés to understand if a prospective mentor has worked exclusively for one organization (often the one sponsoring the mentoring program), or if he or she has experience in different corporate or organizational systems and cultures. The mentor with a significant percentage of his or her career performed at the sponsor organization offers considerable insights into the organization's leadership and their personalities, the corporate culture and its rewards system, political issues that can be tied to career advancement at the organization, and a range of other organization-specific knowledge potentially relevant to the protégé's development needs.

On the other hand, career versatility and employer changes may demonstrate the desirable ability to adapt to different organizations and the people who lead them, or it may show a desirable willingness to take risks in the hopes of accelerating advancement and find opportunities to experience new professional challenges.

3. Special Professional Interests

✳ **Professional Interests to which the Mentor has Dedicated Special Attention.** A title and a resume may not specify to the protégé what special professional interests the mentor has, and what topics or skill sets excite the mentor's interest and curiosity. These special interests may be technical, managerial, research-related, industry-related, or involve a focus on a specialty within the profession that is emerging or is predicted to be of more value in the future. When such special professional interests are clarified, the likelihood increases that an appropriate mentor–protégé match can be created based on shared pursuits and anticipated future professional activities.

A case example: A government sub-agency implements a broad-based mentoring program and asks senior-level managers to complete a Mentor Profile. The agency is undergoing a major transformation of the way it manages information technology services and software development, moving to an Agile-based development process. A Program Manager within the agency has dedicated the past 18 months to studying, receiving training, and achieving certification as a Scrum Master and an Agile Project Manager. The Agile software development technique requires both new development techniques and, as importantly, a willingness to embrace a paradigm shift to greater user involvement and shorter sprints that accelerate the development process. The Program Manager becomes a champion of the new processes being used at the agency, evangelizing the value and success of the

Agile methods. In filling out his Mentor Profile, he emphasizes his special interest in Agile software development and the "scrum" approach. This draws the interest of many junior developers who recognize the importance that Agile processes will play in their immediate and longer-term career.

4. Personal Interests

Rapport is essential in a successful mentoring relationship, and rapport-building between mentor and protégé may have little to do with shared professional interests and more to do with interests outside of work or one's professional career. Bonding can be accelerated by shared interests in politics (for example, active roles in supporting a particular party or movement); professional sport rooting interests (for example, both having season tickets to the regional sports franchise's home games); fitness (for example, both attend the same gym, or both participate in events such as marathons); blogging within shared communities of interest, and so on.

With rapport accelerated by these shared interests, the mentor and protégé have a sound basis for discussions of the protégé's professional needs and aspirations. A danger exists here, though, that when the outside interests are the focus of the discussions within the mentor–protégé relationship, true mentoring may not occur. Both mentors and protégés have a responsibility to get down to business during mentoring encounters, to ensure that mentoring goals are identified, assessed, and pursued on an ongoing basis.

Other Methods Organizations Apply to Support Mentor Selection by Protégés

When establishing a formal mentoring program and culture within an organization, human capital managers face the challenge of facilitating mentoring relationships in a way that simulates more naturally developed, informal pairings that are far more successful, efficient, and enjoyable for the participants. Making the type of Mentor Profile data just discussed available to prospective protégés is a valuable initial step because it provides useful information upon which protégés can make initial mentor down-selections.

The organization must establish a culture that makes the protégé's outreach to a selected mentor a valued, affirmed, and reinforced activity. Furthermore, an active communication program is essential as a mentoring program is established. This communication program should explain the value the organization places on learning from others within the organization, and that mentoring is advocated at all levels of the organization. The primary message to reinforce is that *the organization values the knowledge assets that exist within the organization*, and it advocates leveraging these assets through a mentoring program.

But how to best encourage protégés to actually reach out to the mentors they've chosen in order to begin the mentoring process? Some protégés are likely to hesitate if required to initiate the pairing of their own volition. They may never have met or had substantive interaction with a mentor who appeals to them in a Mentor Profile, and the act of picking up the phone or typing an e-mail requesting assistance of the selected mentor can be as awkward as asking a girl for a first date or to go to the prom. However, the alternative—forcing pairings through a coercive process with implicit penalties for not doing so—rarely works. The essential voluntary nature of mentoring makes any mandates or forced selections counterproductive.

Because voluntarism is the prevailing dynamic in building mentoring relationships, some human capital managers arrange a "mixer" event—an environment in which the spirit of choice is retained, but protégés and mentors at least have an opportunity to meet with each other. This environment is more like speed dating than an unstructured cocktail party. The premise behind it is that, as quirky as such an event might seem in an organizational setting, it enables protégé and mentor to feel each other out and gain a sense of each other's personalities and interests, and it allows intuitive judgments to be made about whether a mentoring relationship might work. Indeed, mentor–protégé pairing is always a highly intuitive process, built on an interpersonal attraction between the parties, so why not allow protégés to meet prospective mentors in a structured setting and encourage both parties to apply their intuition to the selection process?

At this event, mentors are seated at various locations around a large conference room, with another, empty seat opposite them. Signage indicates who they are. Protégés arrive at this setting with a list of down-selected prospective mentors to meet and hold a short discussion. Human capital managers can serve as facilitators to create schedules for the brief discussions between mentor and protégé, and address issues such as certain prospective mentors being too much in demand.

The Mentor's Perspectives: Attributes of a Well-Matched Protégé

What about you as a prospective mentor? What should you be looking for in a mentee or protégé? Despite the fact that the protégé may drive the initial process of selecting a mentor, at least in a formal mentoring context, you too will certainly have a say in whether the mentoring relationship is likely to take off and really work. In the end, mentoring is always a two-way relationship characterized by a mutual emotional commitment to success. Ideally, an effective mentoring relationship is one in which the mentor is as drawn to the protégé as the protégé is attracted to the mentor.

There are certain key attributes to look for in a prospective mentee. You want a mentee who is:

1. **Motivated.** A mentor wants someone who is motivated to succeed in whatever it is that he or she wishes to explore during the mentoring process. The motives may differ from one individual to another (we discuss protégé motivation more in our Powerful Practice #2), but an inner drive to use the mentoring to better one's circumstances is always a characteristic of suitable protégé.

2. **Time-Committed.** A protégé needs to be able to carve out time in his or her schedule to enable the mentoring to take place. If the potential protégé is not able to commit a meaningful amount of time both to the mentoring interactions and to the follow-up that is required as a result of mentoring recommendations, the time spent mentoring will be inefficient and unlikely to have any type

of impact. Time-wasting is a significant risk to the mentor–protégé relationship, and this risk applies as much to the mentor feeling frustration about the waste of his or her time as it applies to protégé's wondering if the mentoring he or she is receiving has any value or not. Dedicating your own time to providing mentoring support should engender appreciation and gratitude from the protégé. If protégé behavior signals a lack of appreciation or gratitude for your time, it may be an opportune moment to examine whether the mentoring relationship should continue.

3. **Positive and Optimistic.** Mentoring is by its nature an exercise in optimism—it advocates for the lasting benefits of new learning and insights. Conversely, negativity tends to be a self-fulfilling prophesy within the mentoring relationship. If an individual is cynical or invariably pessimistic, the delivery of mentoring is not indicated.

4. **Respectful.** You want a protégé who is respectful of you and the expertise you have gained through your career. Respect for one's mentor is at the very foundation of a successful mentor–protégé relationship. And as per item #2 on this list, you also want a protégé who respects the fact that you are going to be allotting valuable time from your busy schedule to deliver specialized support to him or her. Disrespectful behaviors are really the most potent of relationship-killers during the mentoring process. If evidence of disrespect occurs at any time in the relationship, from initial mutual screening

to later on in the relationship, it is time to raise the idea that the protégé may need to find a different mentor.

5. **Open to Learn from You.** This trait involves the excitement and intrinsic motivation to discover new knowledge and insights, which most children show at early stages of development but which sometimes can dissipate with age. A protégé who self-identifies as a "sponge" of knowledge and shows readiness to learn from the mentor's experience will appreciate the mentoring process far more than one who does not self-identify this same way.

6. **Open to Learn About Him- or Herself, and Expand Self-Awareness.** Mentoring is an exercise in expanding self-awareness. Highly defensive and overly sensitive protégés need not apply! Neither should prospective protégés participate in mentoring if they are closed down to feedback from others. You will not want to work with protégés who consistently impede or deflect discussions focused on the way others respond to them, taking the position that this input is not important or personally offensive to them.

7. **Honest.** Truthfulness and credibility are highly intertwined. Honesty is a core "meta-level" need driving any type of service delivery–based relationship (O'Connell 2008). If information in the mentor–protégé dialogue lacks credibility, then the entire mentoring process becomes disingenuous. When mentors ask protégés a question, about work or personal affairs, they need an honest answer in

order to craft the best ways to respond. When protégés' words lack truthfulness, the mentoring process is essentially over.

8. **Communicative.** The protégé needs to be capable of verbalizing his or her experiences and interests, ideally in a way that enables the mentor to understand them clearly. The mentor can advise the protégé about enhanced communication skills, and serve as a role model for higher levels of vocabulary, but protégés need to be able to carry on a conversation, at the very least.

Summary

The best mentor–protégé matches occur informally—the mentor sees a bit of him- or herself in a more junior professional, and is inclined to deliver wisdom accumulated through the years to support the protégé as perhaps he or she too was supported in a mentoring relationship. In such naturally developing relationships, the terms *mentor* and *protégé* may never even be directly spoken. The relationship just evolves, moves at its own pace, and takes the direction that the two parties desire—most often with superior levels of mutual satisfaction in the process.

Companies that seek to replicate the valuable learning and professional development that occurs when effective informal mentoring takes place may wish to create formalized systems that facilitate mentor–protégé relationship-building. Formal mentoring programs often ask prospective mentors to complete a multifaceted profile to inform prospective protégés of their personal and professional background and interests. To overcome awkwardness or resistance to asking a mentor to provide support for them, protégés and mentors may be asked to participate in a structured mutual interviewing process arranged by the organization—sometimes in a kind of "speed dating" to encourage mentor-protégé matches. Such an event has the advantage of enabling the protégé to move beyond the attraction he or she has simply to the mentor's background and gain a sense of the actual interpersonal rapport he or she may feel quickly when meeting a prospective mentor. In the end, mentoring will only be successful when such rapport occurs, and then is translated into value-adding advisory, sponsorship, teaching, and role-modeling-based interactions.

CHAPTER 5

Mentoring as Both Career and Psychosocial Support

Effective mentoring offers protégés a blend of psychosocial and career-development guidance. Protégés in informal mentoring relationships have reported that their mentors provided more psychosocial support functions than protégés who selected or were matched with mentors within more formal mentoring programs. Similarly, protégés in more formal mentoring programs have reported that the focus of the mentoring tends to be more toward career coaching. If this is so, and if informal mentoring is almost always more successful than formal mentoring, then competencies supporting psychosocial development (rather than limiting one's mentoring focus to "here is how I did it" types of professional instruction) appear to be very relevant. But mentors are not filling a role only of counselor or psychotherapist; protégés want sound advisory assistance about workplace and professional challenges. Consequently, really great mentors offer both.

Research has clearly shown that psychosocial mentoring improves protégés' satisfaction with the mentoring process as well as the commitment they have to the organizational environment where they and their mentors operate. (Kagans and Wood, 1999) Why? Because receiving effective mentoring feels good. And if such a positive affective response occurs within an organizational setting, the protégé will connect the experience to being a member of the organization. Therefore, effective mentoring and staff retention are highly related, when the mentors and protégés work for the same organization.

So what is psychosocial mentoring, and why is it an important component of succeeding in the mentor role?

Psychosocial mentoring, or psychosocial support, addresses aspects of the relationship that enhance the protégé's sense of competence, identity, emotional comfort in a meaningful relationship, and pride in growing effectiveness in a professional role. The functions of psychosocial mentoring represent a deeper, more intense mentoring relationship and often depend more on relationship quality than on career function. Because mentors provide their protégés with psychosocial support and opportunities for development, they contribute to the general satisfaction of protégés above and beyond the extrinsic rewards they can secure for their protégés. At its core, mentoring is not about facilitating more earning power, but about creating an exchange of different types of currencies—the ones that are intangible but highly valuable, such as self-fulfillment, pride, learning, and personal growth.

Psychosocial mentoring includes intrinsic functions such as personal acceptance of protégés, without prejudice or condescension based on the protégés' shortcomings or blemishes. Protégés do not need to show off or act as if they need to be perfect to gain their mentors' approval. Actually, the opposite is the case: Effective mentoring occurs in the context of self-awareness of challenges and shortcomings upon which mentoring can focus. A protégé without self-perceived flaws does not need a mentor at all. Fortunately, if you understand the characteristic imperfection of all human beings, mentors are not likely to encounter such an individual!

When protégés rate their mentors retrospectively on the more valuable aspects of their relationship, they often indicate that their mentor demonstrated many relationship-enhancing psychosocial behaviors. These include:

* ❊ Friendship characteristics
* ❊ Social characteristics
* ❊ Parental characteristics
* ❊ Role modeling
* ❊ Counseling

Friendship Characteristics

In an effective mentor–protégé relationship, protégés deem their mentor as someone they can confide in, as someone who provides them with support and encouragement, and as someone they can trust. These friendship-defining attributes distinguish mentoring from other helping professionals who might be inclined to distance themselves from being perceived as a friend, due to professional/personal boundary and appropriateness issues (for example, as a teacher, a therapist, or a supervisor). In contrast to the wariness some helping professionals have of being perceived as a friend while performing their helping role, mentors *embrace* the characteristics of friendship. Effective mentors want to demonstrate they have a stake in their protégés' well-being, and will care about and be available to their protégés regardless of difficult circumstances—much as a close friend would.

Case example: An article in the July 14, 2014 edition of *USA Today* (Joey Gallo Wows Fans in Future Games, by Paul White; USA Today Sports, July 14, 2014) portrays the role of psychosocial mentoring well. It reports that during a recent off-season, minor league slugger Joey Gallo had asked major leaguer Jason Giambi to help him with his hitting and swing at the batting cages Giambi owned in Las Vegas, Nevada. "He took time out of his day every day just to meet with me and to hit with me," Gallo said. "It was great. We talked about everything you could: family, stuff outside of baseball. It's not just baseball. We have lives, too. The things he has been through. So, he was really good at mentoring the mental side and, obviously, hitting too."

Social Characteristics

In effective mentor–protégé pairing, the two often get together informally after work by themselves, may socialize one on one outside the work setting, and frequently have one-on-one, informal social interactions. Mentoring transcends day-to-day work responsibilities; as we noted earlier, it involves offline interactions and support. As one mentor stated to us, "If you wouldn't invite your protégé to join you at a ballgame or professional networking party, your relationship with them cannot really be characterized as mentoring—an advisor or coach maybe, but not a mentor."

Parental Characteristics

As we noted in Chapter 1, there is a parental flavor to most effective mentoring. Protégés who have experienced great mentoring often consider their mentor almost as a father/mother to them, or at least as someone who reminds them of one of their parents. Developing potential and caring are essentials of parenting, so it is not surprising that much overlap exists between the mentor and parent roles.

Role-Modeling

Being a role model is a defining characteristic of mentoring. (We discuss more about the role-modeling aspects of mentoring in Powerful Practice #1.) In general, in effective mentor–protégé relationships, protégés are likely to experience their mentors as individuals whose behaviors they wish to emulate. They see the positive results of behaviors demonstrated by their mentors, and hope they too can engender such responses from others because of the inevitable benefit these types of responses would have on their professional career.

Counseling

Any human interaction between two people character-ized by empathic listening and a shared focus on enhancing self-awareness (the core principles and aptitudes of mentoring we advocated in Chapter 2) is likely to have a counseling component. The counselor (mentor) seeks to understand and respond to the unique circumstances of another (our definition of empathy)—in this case, the protégé. The counselor role includes serving as a sounding board focused on helping the protégé develop and understand him- or herself. The counselor role could also pertain to relationships and behaviors in the workplace. Mentors counsel about how to best respond to certain stimuli and people, providing advice but encouraging the counseling recipient (the protégé) primarily to gain an understanding of the dynamics at play prior to determining any specific course of action.

Mentors providing psychosocial support seek to guide the protégés' personal development as much as their professional development, because they go hand in hand. Each of the 9 Powerful Practices of Really Great Mentors involves the development of personal skills that transcend work competencies. The premise is that the better and more confident a person a protégé becomes, the more successful a professional he or she will be. Psychosocial mentoring activities support the development of protégés' character, credibility, empathy, and interpersonal understanding—all of which are characteristics that research demonstrates time and again are the best indicators of future professional success.

———

Effective mentors integrate career coaching and sponsoring activities with a keen understanding of what the protégé needs most. Mentors are career advocates, and performing such advocacy requires seasoned knowledge about what the relevant profession requires. If mentors want to be rated highly on the value of their career coaching, they must address the following functions:

※ Sponsorship and exposure opportunities

※ Coaching and exposure

※ Coaching and protection

※ Creating customized challenges

Sponsorship and Exposure Opportunities

Well-selected mentors are in a unique position to help their protégés gain exposure to people who are influential in determining protégés' career paths. Judgment is a prerequisite for mentors engaging in such sponsorship or advocacy activities, because the mentors' credibility is at stake in these potential sponsorship or advocacy situations.

Case example: An administrator of a human services agency hires a bright, motivated young professional for a mid-level program-management position. This professional has academic credentials, but not a great deal of professional experience performing in such a role. The program over which this junior manager assumes control requires considerable professional networking and community outreach, because the program's services interface with a wide range of other human services in the region. The administrator takes time to mentor the junior manager at many opportunities. One of the community outreach roles the agency administrator performs is leading a committee sponsored by the city's United Way, addressing the coordination of services for adolescents. Adolescent services are not explicitly related to the program the junior professional leads, but the agency administrator uses his influence to nominate the junior professional to join the committee. The administrator sees the committee as a valuable means for the junior manager to observe how such inter-agency efforts are organized, and to meet managers of other human service organizations. The junior manager appreciates the exposure offered by the committee, and takes advantage of his committee membership to establish linkages with other agencies that result in enhanced growth and community service coordination within the program he leads.

The agency administrator in the case example might have deemed his actions in exposing the junior manager/protégé at his agency to other committee members as a risk, given that most other committee members were far more senior than the protégé. But the committee environment offered many mentoring opportunities: role-modeling a complex team effort, establishing professional connections, and gaining an understanding of the political and interpersonal aspects of service coordination within a community. Consequently, the risks in introducing the protégé were offset by numerous potential rewards. And the sponsorship effort was one the mentor could keep an eye on, and even control if issues arose.

Mentors by definition have a broader sphere of influence than their protégés. This fact is based on the more extensive experience in a profession mentors invariably have, and the seniority of individuals with whom mentors tend to interface. Effective mentors leverage the network they have developed through the years to the advantage of their protégés. Possessiveness about one's professional network or keeping valuable professional contacts away from protégés is not in the spirit of effective mentoring. Mentoring is an exercise in sharing, and allowing a protégé access to what the mentor has developed on his or her own.

Coaching and Exposure

Coaching blends direct instruction with motivation to perform at a higher level. The schoolteacher at the chalkboard writing mathematic equations for students to copy and absorb is not coaching. But an interaction between teacher and student that maps out how a critical function is performed, followed by the teacher offering support during subsequent student performance *is* coaching, especially if it includes discussion about methods to improve performance. Mentors deliver coaching about technical aspects of organizational performance, especially those that can earn appreciation and admiration from others around the protégé.

One way mentors coach their protégés is by facilitating exposure to different people, processes, perspectives, and networks to which the protégé would otherwise not have access.

Case example: A large company's Vice President of Human Resources has an extensive staff, including a large recruitment workforce to fill a range of open positions within the organization. One recruiter is particularly predisposed and hungry to learn both the technical and interpersonal nuances of recruiting for positions to support government contracts, which often involves careful screening of candidates' suitability for special security clearances. The VP sees the value of having one of her recruiters become a Subject Matter Expert about recruiting for government contracting work at agencies requiring various levels of security clearances. The recruiter makes it evident to the VP that he is seeking a mentor to advance his knowledge, skills, and professional career. The VP recommends that the recruiter contact the company's senior security officer, a gentleman who is close to retirement age but remains valuable to the organization because of his extensive knowledge of methods to support timely approvals at Government agencies for different types of security clearances.

The recruiter reaches out to the senior security officer and requests his help in learning the various processes and procedures associated with staff obtaining the required security clearances. The senior security officer points the recruiter to materials and sources of information the officer has gathered through the years about how different agencies conduct suitability approvals to work in an environment where access to different types of information, classified and unclassified, is part of performing in a contractor role. The officer also begins to mentor the recruiter about special interviewing techniques to screen out candidates who are unlikely to be approved for security clearances. The officer role-plays interviews to demonstrate the points he is making. He also mentors the recruiter about ways to teach others to perform effective screening and interviewing of prospective job candidates, from the perspective of their fit at different government agencies to which the security officer has been exposed through the years. The mentoring relationship continues for several years, even after the security officer has officially retired.

The mentor in this case example applies his knowledge and insights to his protégé's professional interests to craft a coaching approach that suggests different strategies to achieve the learning outcomes the protégé is seeking. In the end, the mentoring adds more value by facilitating a process in which the protégé can, in turn, coach others. By transforming the protégé from a student into a coach of others, the mentor adds lasting value for both the protégé and the organization as a whole.

Coaching and Protection

Effective mentors anticipate the challenges their protégés will face, and help them avoid unnecessary pitfalls. In the senior-security-officer-as-mentor case example we just described, the mentor might reach out to contacts he has established at a particular government agency as the recruiter begins to support staffing for a particular contract to be performed at that agency. Leveraging this relationship with the government contact, the mentor can facilitate an introduction of mentor to the contact, and run interference about any new or unique requirements to which the recruiter must comply. The protection function of a mentor must be applied selectively, with the protégé's survival and opportunities for advancement driving the decision to perform such protection activities.

Creating Customized Challenges

The coaching aspect of mentoring follows the forward-thinking perspective made famous by Robert Kennedy when he paraphrased George Bernard Shaw's play *Back to Methuselah*: "There are those that look at things the way they are, and ask *Why?* I dream of things that never were, and ask *Why not?*" Mentors need to ask, "Why not?" and create challenges to the protégé's status quo. Again, the coaching role integrates instruction and motivation. For protégés' intent on quantum leaps in their professional aptitudes and career opportunities, mentoring must pose challenges that are difficult to attain but reap substantial rewards in the process of attaining them. We discuss more about this mentoring function in Powerful Practice #3.

Summary

Effective mentoring involves support for protégés at both the personal and professional level. Learning focused *only* on an individual's career is probably better characterized as coaching, whereas mentoring tends to blend in various psychosocial types of support and guidance.

To help in the understanding of which behaviors characterize mentoring, researchers have used the following measures that define psychosocial and career coaching roles so integral to superior mentoring (Kagans and Cotton 1999).

Psychosocial Mentoring Characteristics

Friendship

My mentor...

- is someone I can confide in.
- provides support and encouragement.
- is someone I can trust.

Social

My mentor...

- and I frequently get together informally after work by ourselves.

- and I frequently socialize one on one outside the work setting.
- and I frequently have one-on-one, informal social interaction.

Parental

My mentor...

- is like a father/mother to me.
- reminds me of one of my parents.
- treats me like a son/daughter.

Role-Modeling

My mentor...

- serves as a role model for me.
- is someone I identify with.
- represents who I want to be.

Counseling

My mentor...

- serves as a sounding board for me to develop and understand myself.
- guides my professional development.
- guides my personal development.

Accepting

My mentor...

- accepts me as a competent professional.
- sees me as being competent.
- thinks highly of me.

Career Development Mentoring Characteristics

Sponsorship

My mentor...

- helps me attain desirable positions.

- uses his/her influence to support my advancement in the organization.

- uses his/her influence in the organization for my benefit.

Coaching

My Mentor...

- helps me learn about other parts of the organization.

- gives me advice on how to attain recognition in the organization.

- suggests specific strategies for achieving career aspirations.

Protection

My mentor...

- protects me from those who may be out to get me.

- runs interference for me in the organization.

- shields me from damaging contact with important people in the organization.

Creating Challenges

My mentor...

- gives me tasks that require me to learn new skills.

- provides me with challenging assignments.

- assigns me tasks that push me to develop new skills.

Exposure

My mentor...

- helps me be more visible in the organization.
- creates opportunities for me to impress important people in the organization.
- brings my accomplishments to the attention of important people in the organization.

If you can effectively adapt your mentoring approach to the variable needs of a protégé at different points in time, all of these functions will be applied. The art of mentoring is knowing when and how to implement such an integrated approach to your teaching, advising, role-modeling, and sponsorship role.

The 9 Powerful Practices of Really Great Mentors that we present next are components of the "artfulness" of truly effective mentoring. As you will see, they apply to both psychosocial and career coaching roles performed by the mentor—at times, within the same practice.

The **9** Powerful Practices
of Really Great Mentors

CHAPTER 6

———◆———

Powerful Practice #1 of
Really Great Mentors:

Model Emotional Intelligence

We defined mentoring as an activity that involves modeling behaviors that are valuable for a protégé to emulate. Modeling is an interpersonal dynamic involving what psychologist Albert Bandura referred to as social learning theory. Bandura posited that people can learn new information and behaviors by watching other people, rather than by simply experiencing reinforcement from others. He labeled this phenomenon "observational learning." (see *http://psychology.about.com/od/developmentalpsychology/a/sociallearning.htm*)

To be a really great mentor, you need to understand that you are being watched by your protégé. Your actions are likely to provide as much—if not more—guidance than the words exchanged between you. Being an effective role model begins

97

with understanding that your behaviors have tremendous influence on what your protégé is learning. When protégés observe certain behaviors and traits in their mentor that they find admirable and then link these behaviors to professional success, they will want to integrate them into their own behavioral repertoire.

If mentors understand that they must be role models for their protégés, it begs the question, What behaviors should mentors try to model for their protégés? Certainly, some modeled behaviors show how to approach a technical challenge often posed within the relevant profession, and mentors teach and practice methodologies that have proven effective in creating more desirable outcomes. For example, a mentor may model behaviors that demonstrate how to run a team meeting effectively, such as always having a meeting agenda and managing the meeting's time closely to ensure the full agenda is discussed.

Mentors' ability to solve technical challenges is clearly important, but a growing body of research demonstrates that what people admire most in others involves not their technical acumen but instead a set of integrated interpersonal skills that, when combined, are best defined as "emotional intelligence." So if you want to be an effective mentor, you need to model behaviors that promote effective *self-awareness*, *self-management*, *relationship awareness*, and *relationship management*.

Emotional intelligence applies to the ability to perceive, control, and evaluate emotions, to discriminate among these perceived emotions, and, perhaps most importantly, to use this information to guide one's thinking and actions. Mentors need to understand the value of this ability, and demonstrate it routinely in all types of circumstances. The skills integral to emotional intelligence relate to being comfortable with both rational and emotional interactions. If mentors are uncomfortable with the latter, they will be unable to apply the proper blend of psychosocial and career guidance, emotional support, and technical coaching we described earlier.

In his book *Emotional Intelligence*, Daniel Goleman wrote that when we work, we are applying both our emotional and rational minds: "These two minds, emotional and rational, operate in tight harmony for the most part, intertwining their different ways of knowing to guide us through the world. Ordinarily there is a balance between the emotional and rational minds, with emotion feeding into and informing the operations of the rational mind, and the rational mind refining and sometimes vetoing the inputs of the emotions." The mentor must understand this dynamic of brain function, and demonstrates to the protégé all the capabilities outlined in Goleman's model. On the following page is a chart that details this model.

Modeling Self-Awareness

Self-awareness is a core competency for mentors because it aligns so significantly with the process mentors try to establish with protégés: the need to conduct an accurate self-assessment, which then guides how to develop one's full potential. Mentoring is about creating an environment for an ongoing examination of the protégés' strengths and career development challenges. The Mentoring Plan the two of you develop together can only have direction and purpose if both parties share a mutual awareness of vital skills that require attention and improvement. Mentoring identifies blind spots that have eluded the protégé's awareness.

Daniel Goleman's Model of Emotional Intelligence

	Self	Awareness
Awareness	Emotional self-awareness	Empathy
	Accurate self-assessment	Developing potential in others
	Core beliefs and values known	Service orientation
	Self-confience	Awareness of "political" currents
Management	Stress management	Conflict management
	Self-control	Building instrumental bonds
	Drive to achieve	Developing potential in others
	Adaptability	Influence/persuasion
	Optimism	Understanding how to add value

Modeling self-awareness requires that mentors be open about how they have expanded their own self-awareness and addressed their own blind spots. Disclosure of this type of information candidly and without defensiveness demonstrates to protégés that the mentor abides by and has grown professionally by embracing the empowering aspects of self-awareness.

Here's an example. **Mentor:** "My blind spot used to be that I thought I managed conflict well, but in actuality I often avoided it or looked the other way to keep from having to engage the other person with whom I had a conflict. One day my boss pulled me aside and said, 'John, this thing you have going on with Jim in quality control is bogging us down. You have to deal with the issue you have with him, and find a resolution. We have a lot of important things to worry about, and Jim's conflict with you should not be one of them.' So here I was thinking I had arbitrated a working understanding with this fellow to get us past our differences, but in reality he continued to sabotage what I and my team were trying to do. I had blinders on, I wanted to believe I had solved the problem, but in retrospect, I knew I had not. So I took the blinders off, and took Jim on, head to head. There was no other way—I had to find out what our real differences were, and get them sorted out so they did not interfere with my group's work."

This type of self-disclosure demonstrates that often the factor holding someone back professionally is not in having interpersonal challenges at work—who doesn't?—but in failing to have awareness about what these challenges reflect about oneself. When protégés hear about how self-awareness contributed to greater insight, which in turn contributed to greater control over relevant challenges at work, they understand the significant value of self-knowledge ultimately contributing to behaviors that advance professional success.

One method mentors can easily model is expanding one's self-awareness by seeking feedback. Mentors can ask their protégés for feedback about *anything*, from what they are wearing that day to how they came across in a presentation the protégé witnessed. Seeking feedback models a behavior that shows openness to gathering information that can build valuable self-awareness. Every day offers new opportunities to expand self-awareness about a range of factors impacting professional growth. It is as simple as asking for opinions about how you are perceived by others, which you may or may not accept as gospel truth. But soliciting more data about the perceptions of others is always valuable in and of itself—accepted or not.

Modeling *emotional* self-awareness—understanding what you are *feeling*, and why—offers many additional benefits:

* Demonstrating a comfort level with reflecting feelings to enhance understanding

* Encouraging protégés to build their "emotional radar" in interactions with others, which facilitates developing a greater comfort level with emotion-laden situations

* Improving self-management skills (discussed next), because emotional self-awareness engenders emotional self-control

Mentors who personify this connection from emotional self-awareness to enhanced self-control are excellent role models for their protégés.

Modeling Self-Management

Self-management skills include managing stress effectively, keeping potentially disruptive emotions and impulses in check, maintaining the drive to achieve, adapting to new circumstances, and manifesting optimism even amid difficult periods. By modeling these self-management competencies, the mentor demonstrates how effective leaders operate: they manage their stress levels, eliminate or modulate self-defeating impulses, cope with changes, and remain positive when others are prone to complain or express negativity. Leaders manage themselves to be more effective in managing others.

If the mentor and protégé work together in the same organization or environment, the likelihood exists that a) stressors will occur, b) both mentor and protégé will be exposed to similar stressors, and c) self-management skills to cope with these commonly experienced stressors are relevant to discussions within the mentor–protégé relationship about the protégé's professional growth. For example, change may be inducing a stressful environment at work. Perhaps roles will be changing inside the organization, or external factors such as customer demands may be engendering the stressful conditions. Whereas circumstances in the environment may be out of the control of both mentor and protégé, how each person responds to the stressful circumstance is within the individual's control.

Mentors need to demonstrate the self-control to not allow stressful circumstances to create what is called "emotional hijacking." When emotionally hijacked, individuals cannot think straight. They tend to devolve into reactive responses that are induced by the limbic system, the brain's emotion factory that creates the chemical messages that connect information to memory. When experiencing a danger or stressor, our brains can get flooded with emotional messages tied to "fight or flight" decision-making. The result of this brain chemistry is fear, confusion, anxiety, and often cognitive paralysis. In this circumstance, individuals are not in control—their limbic system is.

But humans have the more advanced neocortex component of the brain that enables us to reason and think through difficult situations, and mitigate the limbic system's potentially hijacking messages. We experience a threat, live through it, learn from it, and allow our neocortex brain function to support more wise and mature responses to potential similar threats in the future. We condition ourselves to use our heads when stressed.

Mentors can be highly influential as models of such neocortex-enabled maturity in response to stressors. The methods that mentors model to manage stress can vary. Some manage stress by emphasizing patience, whereas others choose to take action. Some increase their exercise regimen, whereas others choose to chill out in whatever way induces mental relaxation for them. Some want to build awareness by analyzing the stressful circumstance, whereas others elect to allow the circumstances to play out before conducting such an analysis. No matter the method of dealing with stress, the main attribute mentors need to model is not allowing oneself to be emotionally hijacked by the environment or circumstances. Mentors who convey such calm and capabilities to manage stress effectively show their protégés how to think straight amid stressful or even chaotic situations.

Mentors also need to model optimism. It's easy to get caught up in pessimistic cognitions about one's organization, department, leadership team, and so on, but effective mentorship is delivered from an optimistic perspective of the status quo and future. It is often the path less traveled; people tend to complain and find fault in an environment of stress. Open-ended questioning by mentors about how the protégé might use the stressful situation to his or her advantage can be valuable. It forces the protégé to consider more "glass half full" perspectives about the circumstances. Leadership is an exercise in optimism amid risks that play out in a number of ways. Mentors need to show their protégés how important it is to curb pessimistic impulses and lead with the attitude that risks are inevitable, and they can be effectively mitigated if given sufficient problem-solving attention. The message that the enterprise can emerge from the stressful circumstances stronger and with more robust capabilities is important to convey.

Modeling Relationship Awareness

In Chapter 2 we discussed how seeking first to understand—a major contributor to building relationship awareness—is a core skill for mentors. Relationship awareness requires practicing empathy, reading situations and relationship dynamics, and cultivating a "service orientation"—that is, the ability to put oneself inside others' frameworks or perspectives and respond as one would want to be treated. The Golden Rule is always a valuable framework upon which to model behaviors in the mentor–protégé relationship.

Relationship awareness also breeds understanding of the "political" aspects of behaviors inside the enterprise. Individuals with keen relationship awareness open their emotional sensors to others around them, and create perceptions about how certain behaviors are rewarded and penalized by the organization.

Mentors may choose to introduce relationship awareness issues with protégés by initiating a discussion about the protégés' "take" on certain relationships they have at work. After exploring their protégés' perspectives, mentors may choose to reveal how they perceive the same circumstances, and how they have developed this perception. Here's an example.

Mentor: "Based on what you are telling me and what I have observed, my sense is that your boss is a 'make me look good and I will take care of you too' type of manager. She may be a bit unsure of her place in the overall management structure and needs some wins to bolster her image. For you, her approach fits in well with behaviors that you are prone to show, like looking to share the credit for victories within the team, even when you have done most of the heavy lifting. Tell me if that rings true for you, and if it does, what does it mean for how you will approach the project you are working on currently?"

The mentor has modeled making interpretations about relationship issues pertinent to the protégé, emphasizing emotional aspects of relationship-building behaviors. After modeling relationship awareness skills, the mentor elicits more understanding from the protégé about better managing his or her relationship with the boss. The behavior being modeled is, in essence, relationship-awareness-engendering methods to gain better control over highly instrumental business relationships.

At times, relationship awareness is a skill that needs some practice. Protégés may prefer to remain focused on a specific task they are performing and its many components rather than focusing on the relationships that make accomplishing the task easier. Mentors strive to make protégés comfortable with the idea that relationships are critical to their success and their achievement of future aspirations. Often, it is the interpersonal capabilities shown in a collaborative effort that propel a protégé upward on a career path, even more than possessing the technical skills to get the task done well.

Modeling Relationship Management

Mentoring in and of itself models relationship management, because a core element of this emotionally intelligent skill is developing potential in others. So, when protégés perceive the value-adding behaviors a mentor uses to develop their potential, they are observing effective relationship management in action.

Relationship management skills are tested by the experience of conflict with others. Conflict undermines relationships and creates the type of interpersonal discord that can make performing one's job a supreme challenge. Mentors can model the concept that conflict can be managed, and that often, conflict offers opportunities for improving instrumental relationships throughout a longer period of time. Such modeling of conflict-management skills can occur in the actual mentoring process—a mentor's insight or recommendation may create a negative emotional reaction from the protégé that engenders conflict in the relationship. Mentors can then model conflict-management skills by finding out the true nature of the conflict with the protégé, and by showing understanding about the protégé's position before trying to discover a way to resolve the dispute. As importantly, the mentor can promote an approach to conflict that tries to focus on the issues, not the personalities or behaviors that are simply an offshoot of being in a state of conflict. If the mentor and protégé can resolve their own conflicts, then the protégé has an effective model from which to approach future interpersonal conflicts at work.

Mentoring can also involve finding opportunities to sponsor the protégé in some way, such as facilitating the protégé's ability to network with a broader sphere of influence. The actions associated with sponsoring the protégé demonstrate the importance of nurturing instrumental relationships to advance professionally. Protégés observe the value in spending time and resources establishing and developing relationships with those who can provide support to them in the future.

How emotionally intelligent are you now, as you read this book on mentoring effectiveness? It is an important question, certainly. You cannot model behaviors that are not part of your repertoire. You cannot show how to be smart about your emotions if you struggle with the emotional aspects of your life or job. Tests exist to measure one's emotional IQ, known as "EQ," and you might want to pursue these in order to gain a sound understanding of just how emotionally intelligent you really are. But here are a group of characteristics you can assess yourself against now, as you read this book, to gain a sense of whether you need considerable or just refresher training on EQ skills.

* You tend to be curious, including about people you do not know. You ask questions of others, rather than framing the interaction by focusing on yourself.

* You are a good leader, because you understand the importance of people management (you can

read our other book, *9 Powerful Practices of Really Great Bosses*, to learn what can make you most effective as a people manager).

✳ You know your strengths and weaknesses, and perform work with this understanding. Self-awareness breeds confidence.

✳ You know how to pay attention. Goleman writes, "Your ability to concentrate on the work you are doing...is a strong predictor of your success..." (Goleman 1995).

✳ When you feel a strong emotion, you understand why you are feeling it. Knowing what you are feeling and why helps modulate the deleterious effects of emotional hijacking, a phenomenon we often see when people blow up inappropriately or become extremely depressed by circumstances around them.

✳ You can get along with most people. You adapt to different people to build rapport (more on that later, in Powerful Practice #3).

✳ You read people, and respond accordingly. You can also "read a room"; that is, you are able to gain a rapid sense of the mood within a team or group.

✳ You are relatively resilient, and optimistic. When you fall, you soon get back up and plod ahead.

✳ You trust your gut; that is, your intuition that is fed by emotional awareness, both of others and within yourself.

Summary

The practice of modeling emotional intelligence is intrinsic to building the mentor's credibility and worth as an advisor and teacher. Each of the four major components of building a higher EQ is relevant for mentors to model for their protégés.

1. **Self-awareness.** Some modeling behaviors for mentors to have in their repertoire include:

    ✳ Sharing experiences with protégés about how you have constructively addressed your own blind spots

    ✳ Seeking feedback, from the protégé and while the protégé is observing you at work, to demonstrate the value of and widespread opportunities for integrating the perceptions of others into your awareness of personal strengths and challenges

    ✳ Conducting an ongoing effort to maintain an accurate self-assessment—this provides a model for protégés to emulate as the Mentoring Plan is developed and implemented

2. **Self-management.** Some modeling behaviors for mentors to have in their repertoire include:

    ✳ Managing your stress level effectively, in whatever way works best for you. Protégés often need to observe effective methods for coping with stress, either to emulate or to prompt considerations about what would work best for them in managing their stress

- ※ Conveying the value of thinking straight and using your head when confronted with risks or challenges, avoiding emotional hijacking
- ※ Remaining optimistic—note opportunities and "glass half full" perspectives that exist amid the process of experiencing difficulties

3. **Relationship awareness.** Some modeling behaviors for mentors to have in their repertoire include:
   - ※ Following Golden Rule principles, treating others (including the protégé) as you would wish to be treated
   - ※ Putting yourself in the protégé's place to gain greater understanding of his or her perspectives
   - ※ Seeking first to understand, before trying to be understood
   - ※ Addressing relationships in discussions of task performance, to model how awareness adds value both to the task and to professional development planning
4. **Relationship management.** Some modeling behaviors for mentors to have in their repertoire include:
   - ※ Developing potential in others, including but not necessarily limited to the protégé
   - ※ Managing conflict by differentiating the respective positions in the conflict before trying to achieve resolution

  ❋ Advocating that opportunities can emerge
    from conflicts

  ❋ Nurturing your instrumental relationships,
    and using these relationships in protégé spon-
    sorship opportunities

CHAPTER 7

Powerful Practice #2 of Really Great Mentors:

Initially, Explore Intrinsic and Extrinsic Motivation

Different protégés will have different motivations to engage in a mentoring relationship. Mentors can never begin a relationship with a protégé with presumptions about what the best outcomes will be for that individual. It is best to start with an open slate, and let the story unfold about just what the protégé's motivation is to learn and receive guidance from you as a mentor.

Certainly, both immediate and longer-term goals are important for the mentor to identify—at some point. But in the initial stages of the relationship, the focus should be on understanding what excites the protégé about his or her future prospects. This second powerful practice of mentoring demonstrates how to go about assessing and uncovering the motivational forces within protégés, which will have a significant impact on your mentoring approach.

Intrinsic motivation occurs when we act without any obvious external rewards. We simply enjoy an activity or see it as an opportunity to explore, learn, and actualize our potential. For example, you might be reading this book to explore, learn, and develop your potential as a mentor. Consequently, the motivation is to achieve the intrinsic rewards of learning to be as effective as possible performing in the mentoring role. But what if you were placed in a training group at work, and reading this book was mandatory? Then the reward for reading this book—completing the training course and moving on from there—is more extrinsically motivated.

Psychologists Richard M. Ryan and Edward L. Deci describe the construct of intrinsic motivation as an individual's "natural inclination toward assimilation, mastery, spontaneous interest, and exploration that is so essential to cognitive and social development and that represents a principal source of enjoyment and vitality throughout life...[it is] the prototypic manifestation of the human tendency toward learning and creativity" (Ryan and Deci 2000). Psychologists note that children show this human tendency to be intrinsically motivated early in their development. Then the "real world" sets in and we tend to be motivated by a range of other factors: to comply with rules, abide by norms, earn sufficient income through supervised work, and so on. But it is clear that intrinsic motivation is the type that "produces" more. Comparisons between people whose motivation is authentic (they really want to learn new things!) and those who are merely externally controlled for an action (they learn because they have to) typically reveal that the intrinsically motivated have more interest, excitement, and confidence, which in turn is manifested through enhanced performance, persistence, and creativity (Deci and Ryan 1991; Sheldon, Ryan, Rawsthorne, and Ilardi 1997). For mentors, this should just be common sense.

If mentoring is about accelerating the protégé up the learning curve, then mentors are far more able to support rapid learning if their protégés are intrinsically motivated to explore issues or competencies, and are excited to develop their own potential. If they are involved in mentoring through the type of organizationally sponsored mentoring programs described in Chapter 3, then the rewards for participation may not necessarily be intrinsic. The would-be protégés may be there because they have been told to participate.

Consequently, the first question to ask a protégé is the following:

"Why are you here?"

Or, a better way to get to the same set of understandings may be by asking the question slightly differently, from the context of the collaborative aspect of a mentor-protégé relationship:

"Why are *we* here?"

Eliciting motivation in this way is better than the common question most service providers ask: "How can I help you?" That question, besides being overly general, focuses protégés on the mentor as a solution-provider, rather than a facilitator of a self-exploration.

The protégé's response may tend toward aspects of intrinsic motivation: "I am here to grow and learn. I am not sure what that means yet, but I'll know it when I experience it." Or it may tend toward more extrinsically motivated factors: "I am here to get to the next level, whatever that takes." If the protégé speaks of intrinsic rewards, the content will include words like *grow, learn, explore, find out,* and so on. The more extrinsic, reward-focused responses are characterized by words or phrases such as *achieve, deliver, results, make more income,* or *get to where you have gotten.*

It may be tempting to take the time initially to review your background with the protégé, or to explain what you believe can be accomplished through the mentoring process, but it is important to set the "other-oriented" tone from the very beginning. Again, it's not about you. And if it is about the protégé, it is essential to get inside his or her frame of reference from the outset and clarify the motivating factors behind the protégé's involvement in the mentoring relationship. To gain a broader understanding of your protégé's motivations, you can continue to address the defining aspects of intrinsic motivation:

"What excites you or fulfills you in your life? How about at your job, or in practicing your profession?"

Again, assess the response's tending toward more intrinsic or more extrinsic rewards.

"What excites you about your future?"

This assesses if the protégé seeks out opportunities for growth, learning, and development of skills in their future that have broader impacts than simply day-to-day functioning at work, or if the excitement is tied to a set objective with an anticipated extrinsic reward attached to it.

"What happens at a great day at work?"

This reveals whether the protégé finds personal fulfillment through more intrinsic rewards, such as relatedness to others and self-actualizing learning, or if fulfillment from their professional endeavors stems more from receiving an extrinsic reward (for example, a promotion, a salary raise, or a new assignment).

"On a self-motivational scale that begins at zero and ends at 10, what number would you assign yourself if zero was 'Avoids Failure' and 10 was 'Consistently Seeks Exciting New Challenges Even if There are Some Risks Attached'?"

The response gives you a sense of how imperative it is from the protégé's perspective to keep growing and exploring new opportunities even if they involve some risk, versus the more extrinsic, reward-based characteristic to avoid failing at all costs.

Clearly, a mentoring approach to the highly intrinsically motivated protégé will be quite different than the approach to the protégé who is minimally motivated to receive mentoring or is focused on achieving a specific extrinsic reward (or avoiding the punishing aspects of not attaining these rewards). But this is far from being an either/or, black-or-white issue. If intrinsic motivation is a human characteristic, then it may need to be nurtured. It could be lying dormant or idle inside the protégé. Mentors may need to help uncover intrinsic motivation, enabling protégés to see that even with extrinsic rewards in play, they are in charge of their own destiny—not the extrinsic reward only. For example, after posing the prior question about how the protégé rates him- or herself on a risk-avoidance/seeking-challenges scale, you can elicit more information about the self-rating:

"Tell me more about why you gave yourself that rating. Has it ever been different for you? If so, what changed?"

"What would the consequences be if you took a risk and failed?"

The figure on the next page details the real-world notion that most motivation is impacted by extrinsic rewards. Much of the motivational spectrum involves extrinsic rewards, but even with extrinsic rewards evident, you can approach mentoring with the objective of engendering what psychologists refer to as "internal locus of causality." This is a critical understanding for mentors to gain about their protégés: who and what causes the protégé's future to turn out as it will? Does the protégé deem the cause of his or her actions toward achieving a desired future as being driven by external factors and extrinsic rewards? Or does the protégé need assistance in assuming the role of "Chief Life Officer," wherein the locus of control is largely turned self-driven?

For protégés stuck in a motivational pattern driven by extrinsic rewards and perceptions of an external locus of causality, Mentoring Plans may need to be more directive. This is what the protégé seeks: advice and counsel to follow on how to avoid pitfalls and attain a desired reward. The Mentoring Plan for this protégé mirrors a project plan, from project start-up to completion date, with milestones set along the way. Ultimately, it is up to the protégé to execute the plan, but the pathway is well defined by the mentor. When each milestone is attained, the mentor can review the protégé's sense of personal fulfillment in doing so. Often, this review elicits self-actualizing intrinsic rewards from the process of moving forward and making progress.

For protégés driven by developing interests, enjoyment, learning, and satisfaction from achieving a sense of personal fulfillment, the mentor is more likely to be just a facilitator as

Dr. Edward Deci's Model of Intrinsic and Extrinsic Motivation, and its Implications for Mentoring Approaches

Behavior	Nonself - Determined				Self-Determined
Motivation	Amotivation	Extrinsic Motivation			Intrinsic Motivation
Regulatory Styles	Non-Regulation	External Regulation	Introjected Regulation	Identified Regulation	Integrated Regulation	Intrinsic Regulation
Perceived Locus of Causality	Impersonal	External	Somewhat External	Somewhat Internal	Internal	Internal
Relevant Regulatory Processes	Nonintentional, Nonvaluing, Incompetence, Lack of Control	Compliance, External Rewards and Punishments	Self-control, Ego-Involvement, Internal Rewards and Punishment	Personal Importance, Conscious Valuing	Congruence, Awareness, Synthesis With Self	Interest, Enjoyment, Inherent Satisfaction

Mentoring Approach: Directive .... **Promoting Autonomy** ....

opposed to a directive project planner. The Mentoring Plan in this instance is driven by the protégé. The mentor can make suggestions about methods the protégé can apply to achieve greater fulfillment, but the decision whether, when, and where to use these recommended methods is the protégé's. The mentor's focus is less on a reward or milestone, but on the protégé's sense of self-actualization—that he or she is enjoying the process, finding fulfillment, and enjoying the journey more than specifically defined outcomes. When one is on a sound path to reach one's full potential, the desired career outcomes almost invariably follow.

Many protégés will fall in the middle, between these two extremes. They will want guidance about steps to take to achieve an extrinsic reward, but they also want to gain a sense of congruence, awareness, or synthesis between attainment of a milestone and a sense of greater learning and fulfillment. For mentors, it means you must be flexible and adaptable to what protégés are telling you at a particular point in time.

Summary

Protégés manifest a wide range of motivations to participate in a mentoring relationship. A continuum exists, from the unmotivated who feel coerced to participate to the protégé who seeks the simple, almost childlike joy of learning new thing and exploring the meaning of their lives. Mentors who begin the relationship with a protégé by assessing the intrinsic and extrinsic motivation to participate in the relationship are able to craft mentoring strategies aligned with these expressed motivations.

The more the protégé focuses on the power of external rewards (or avoidance of failure) and external locus of control over his or her fate, the more likely it is that a directive mentoring approach will work best. However, as a milestone in the directive plan is approached or attained, the mentor has an opportunity to explore more intrinsic rewards reaped through the process.

Conversely, protégés exhibiting high levels of intrinsic motivation for learning and exploring themselves and how their careers align with personal fulfillment are best supported by mentors focused on protégés' autonomous decision-making and direction of their own plan. Mentors in this case focus less on milestones and more on measures of fulfillment and the joy of learning new things. Intrinsically motivated individuals tend to produce more, and this will positively impact their professional success.

The largest numbers of protégés fall in between these two types: they seek guidance about how to achieve professional milestones, but want to integrate their success in doing so within a framework of learning and personal fulfillment. Attainment of the extrinsic reward can be viewed as the outcome of following a process focused on attaining fulfillment from the work one performs.

CHAPTER 8

———

*Powerful Practice #3 of
Really Great Mentors:*

Build Rapport Through Understanding
of Different People Styles

Mentors and their protégés need not be alike in their personalities or ways of interacting with other people in order to form an effective learning-focused relationship. Indeed, some insist that opposites attract. We may learn far more from someone who approaches professional circumstances from a different perspective and personality type than our own. But can an effective rapport be built within a mentoring relationship when it is composed of people of different interactive styles? Mentors who wish to support a wider variety of potential protégés, without limiting themselves to a specific protégé personality type, need to be aware of methods to enhance rapport when the protégé interacts with others in ways that are far different from their own.

Psychologists have grouped people into four overarching personality styles, with respect to their level of responsiveness and assertiveness with others within their environment (see the figure on the next page):

1. Drivers
2. Expressives
3. Amiables
4. Analyticals

Dorothy and Robert Bolton referred to these groupings as "people styles." Let's review each of these people styles and understand the implications of each for performing in a mentoring role.

Drivers

This style blends higher-than-average assertiveness with lower-than-average responsiveness to others' specialized needs. The Driver people style is:

✳ Very results- and bottom-line-oriented

✳ Very independent

✳ Very decisive

✳ Able to change mindsets easily

✳ Fast-paced and purposeful

✳ Likely to excel at time management

✳ Factual but not detailed; rational but not theoretical; direct and to the point

✳ Able to bulldoze through an agenda he or she prefers

Less

Analytical		Driver	
• Tends to be a perfectionist • Wants to get it right • Systematic & organized • Task-oriented • Decides from data • Prudent as risk-taker	• Likes solitary work • Loyal • Low-key, quiet • Not comfortable with feelings-based discussions • Likes routines • Not candid	• Oriented to results and bottom line • Independent • Decisive • Able to change others' mindsets easily • Fast-paced • Purposeful	• Excels at managing time and scheduling • Factual but not overly detail-oriented • Direct and to the point • Bulldozer as advocate for own agenda
Amiable		Expressive	
• Team player • Tends to affiliate, rather than perform alone • Not a spotlight-seeker • Avoids ego clashes • Seeks and promotes compromise	• Sensitive to feelings • Service-oriented • Values the status quo • Not candid with others • Comfortable with routine • Easygoing, likeable	• Outgoing, flamboyant • Thrives in limelight; likes being center of attention • Restless, energetic • Maintains a strong personal network • Charismatic	• Impulsive, intuitive • Opportunity-driven (not plan-driven) • Playful and fun-loving • Great people skills • Life of the party • Not detailed or task-oriented

More

Responsiveness

Less — **Assertiveness** — **More**

125

Mentoring a Driver

Mentors should be prepared for an aggressive pace of implementing the learning plan for a protégé with a Driver personality. There is likely to be little need to prod the protégé to act. Drivers often possess both intrinsic and extrinsic motivation, and can move their own learning plan autonomously. Consequently, the mentor is most useful as a source of additional information and guidance, which Drivers will accept if it aligns with their purposefulness and clear-cut objectives.

Drivers are results-driven, and may experience some frustration with mentoring not tied directly to the Mentoring Plan's stated objectives. Mentors may need to coax Driver protégés into discussing more personal issues. Psychosocial mentoring may be of less importance to a Driver.

The offline nature of mentoring fits in well with Drivers. They tend to be focused on their work during business hours and have less interest in activities focused on their learning and development, so it may be best to get the Driver away from work to perform mentoring. This enables the discussion to have some psychological air and freedom to move the way it naturally moves. If the "bulldozer" qualities of the Driver manifest themselves in the mentoring process, mentors may need to find ways to pull the plug on the Driver and encourage more of a reflective and well-paced tone to their interactions.

Expressives

People in this quadrant combine a high level of assertiveness with much emotional expression. Expressives tend to:

※ Be the most outgoing and flamboyant of the styles

* Like bright colors, bold statements, and eye-catching projects
* Thrive in the limelight and gravitate to center stage
* Be restless and energetic
* Link up with others in everything they do
* Have a strong personal network
* Be dreamers who are bold and imaginative
* Be impulsive—they act or speak first and think later
* Prefer to work according to opportunities rather than according to plans
* Be playful and fun-loving
* Be more into talking than listening
* Be more people-oriented than task-oriented
* Speak to find out what they are thinking
* Tell it like it is

Mentoring Expressives

The process of mentoring an Expressive requires a comfort level with verbal interchanges about a range of topics, and a need to cope with occasional impulsivity that may derail a carefully constructed Mentoring Plan. Indeed, the mentoring process with an Expressive needs to be highly adaptive to new priorities and interests that may pop up at any time. Expressives tend to be very intrinsically motivated, thus they tend to prefer autonomy in developing and implementing a Mentoring Plan.

Mentors need to pick up the pace verbally and be prepared for light and joking behaviors that reinforce the Expressive's social aptitudes.

Expressives are *very* responsive to psychosocial mentoring. They will want to engender a friendship and create socialization opportunities. Expressives will have no difficulty sharing information about their lives—perhaps to a fault. There may be times when a mentor will need to get the protégé to focus in on work and career issues, when the Expressive would prefer to share anecdotes or speak about other people.

Providing recognition and reinforcement to Expressives is valuable and effective. They respond well to genuine support and applause for their behavior. They enjoy, rather than shun, the limelight.

Mentors will enjoy their time with Expressives. The rapport between the two of you will not be difficult to create, mainly because the Expressive will take the lead in creating it. Expressives are natural rapport-builders. Stay on the Expressive's wavelength and enjoy the banter and give-and-take the relationship will involve.

Amiables

Amiables will tend to be those who:

※ Are team players

※ Prefer working with others on projects, particularly in small groups or with one other partner

※ Do not seek the spotlight and avoid ego clashes

※ Find ways to integrate conflicting ideas

✳ Are easygoing and likeable

✳ Are especially sensitive to other people's feelings

✳ Perform well in service-oriented positions or responsibilities

✳ Value what has been created and strive to preserve it

✳ Are comfortable doing routine procedures and following processes established by others

✳ Are reluctant to "tell it like it is" for fear of alienating others

Mentoring Amiables

The process of mentoring Amiables requires an understanding that compliance with a planned learning opportunity does not always translate into motivation to gain enhanced knowledge or skills—it may be simply a function of the Amiable's need to please you as the mentor. Amiables may need training in how to assert themselves in situations monopolized by Drivers or Expressives, if their career path requires that they demonstrate this type of behavior.

Mentors will like their Amiable protégés on a personal level, but may need to be careful not to let Amiables' likability deter them from confronting passive behaviors that reflect little urgency to realize future advancement and growth. The service orientation of Amiables is likely to draw their mentors' admiration, but they are not as likely to be strategic thinkers. They won't probe as easily into root causality—they would prefer to be part of the solution that has already been developed by others. They get along, but are not likely to drive innovation or creativity. Consequently, mentoring may require encouragement for the Amiable to get outside his or her comfort zone a bit, think more creatively, and be a leader rather than a supporter.

Analyticals

These individuals combine considerable emotional constraint with less than average assertiveness. Analyticals will tend to be those who are:

✳ Perfectionists

✳ Appalled by a "ready, fire, aim" strategy to making decisions

✳ The "get it right" type—they want to be certain of making the correct choice

✳ Systematic, well-organized, and task-oriented

✳ Attracted to data-driven decision-making. The more data, the better.

✳ Very prudent in risk-taking

✳ Comfortable with solitary work and personal activities (staying at home rather than going to a party or after-work get-together, reading books, and so on)

✳ Loyal when the going gets tough

✳ More low-key and quiet; they do not wear their emotions on their sleeve

✳ Likely to lean back in a chair even when making a point.

* People who think about what they are saying as they say it, and even interrupt themselves and begin a new thought that came to mind—a trait that often confuses listeners

* Likely to favor written over spoken communication

* People who intellectualize feelings

* Punctual for appointments but potentially tardy on deadlines.

Mentoring Analyticals

The process of mentoring Analyticals is likely to be plan-driven, because Analyticals prefer to have the learning program written down to review and analyze. Achieving milestones in the Mentoring Plan may serve as opportunities to uncover more intrinsic motivation. Mentors may initially perceive that exponential growth is less important to the Analytical protégé than simply reinforcing the motivation to stay in compliance with an agreed-to plan. Stretch goals may throw off Analytical personalities—they may get too focused on the feasibility of a stretch goal, without seeing the value in having high aspirations or a drive toward new levels of excellence. Mentors need to work through this process of finding more innate motivation to excel and innovate, when Analyticals are prone to see the risks and vulnerabilities of aiming too high.

Mentoring interventions that seek to elicit insights and emotional content from Analyticals are likely to prompt intellectualized expressions of feelings that reflect very little of their inner world. Consequently, mentors can use a more directive approach to mentoring while looking for teaching moments that illustrate the value of enhancing intrinsic motivation to learn and grow.

Analyticals value career coaching more than psychosocial mentoring. The friendship and socialization aspects of psycho-social mentoring do not come as naturally to the Analytical as they do to the Expressive or the Amiable. Consequently, rapport is built around being mutually engaged in a shared plan, which the Analytical fully understands and for which the Analytical wishes to meet pre-set milestones. Mentors are likely to be verbalizing the words, "Okay we're on plan," when discussing the progress being made through the relationship.

Assessing Your Own People Style

Mentors should assess their own people style as well, to un-derstand whether their style is in sync with their protégés' style. When it is, mentors can identify the type of support that would make sense if provided to them. If the mentor's people style is different from his or her protégé's style, then the mentor will need to flex to the different people style by adapting his or her rapport-building approach to the different people style.

Robert Bolton and Dorothy Grover Bolton, authors of *People Styles at Work*, emphasize that "style flex" is a way of adapting to another person's "process," rather than a way to conform to his or her point of view. "Style flex" is goal-oriented; it is intended to build better rapport and thereby manage the relationship. These are highly relevant attributes of a mentor-ing relationship, especially if it was produced formally through an organizational mentoring program with protégés serving as the primary driver of the matching process. Once selected by a protégé in these circumstances, the mentor has little choice but to find ways to facilitate the rapport-building so valuable in the initial stages of the relationship. Style flexing can be a valuable way of doing so.

According to the Boltons, style flex is a "temporary adjustment of a few behaviors to improve the results of an interaction" (Bolton and Bolton 1996). The skill focuses on changing yourself (the part over which you have control), not changing the protégé (over which you have very little control). The primary leverage you have for improving the mentor–protégé relationship is likely to be your own behavior.

Summary

Mentors will be most effective in their relationship with protégés if they build rapport from the initial phase of the mentoring process onward. Building rapport is a natural process that involves the blending of the relationship's personality types. Often, mentors and protégés are quite different in their personality styles, which can add valuable diversity to the relationship. But mentors need to understand the style by which their protégés interact with others, both to build their relationship and to guide protégés in their relationships with others.

Dorothy and Robert Bolton crafted a model of "people styles" that reflect four different personality types, based on human beings' respective levels of assertiveness and responsiveness with others. The four people style designations—Drivers, Expressives, Amiables, and Analyticals—are rather equally represented in the workforce. Mentors need to identify their protégés' people style, and adapt a rapport-building approach based on this understanding. By doing so, mentors accelerate the process of creating a shared emotional commitment to the mentoring process.

CHAPTER 9

*Powerful Practice #4 of
Really Great Mentors:*

Identify and Pursue Stretch Goals

In Chapter 5, we alluded to the limiting nature of focusing only on avoiding punishments or averting professional pitfalls when professional growth is the objective. The concept that greater risks can yield greater reward is fundamental to the mentoring process. Why take a conservative route when performing in the mentoring role, if protégés often move forward in their careers without receiving the guidance of a mentor? To truly add value, the mentor–protégé relationship should be considering dynamic objectives that would represent a significant advancement in skills and competencies. We refer to these objectives as "stretch" goals.

We define stretch goals as those that cannot be achieved by incremental or small improvements but require extending oneself to the very limits of self-actualization. By definition, stretch goals are not reached immediately; rather, they are framed from a longer-term perspective. For example, during GE's golden years, CEO Jack Welch described stretch goals as asking for the almost impossible, which facilitates getting workers to reach beyond what they had previously thought feasible and achieve amazing results.

We often hear about the value of pushing ourselves beyond our presumed limits. For example, an individual rehabbing a leg injury vows not just to recover, but eventually to run a marathon or climb Mount Everest. In one of the most heralded stretch goals ever established, President Kennedy in the early 1960s advocated that within a 10-year period NASA show the capability not just to send a human into space and return the human and spacecraft safely, but to also send humans and spacecraft all the way to the lunar surface and return them safely. At the time that goal was established, it seemed an impossibility. But in 1969, the goal was met.

Companies mirror this process of establishing stretch goals when they craft their vision statements. Here are some examples of vision statements that demonstrate how the company's purpose is aligned significantly with the concept of establishing and striving for stretch goals:

* **SRA International:** "SRA aspires to be the world's best company in everything we do."

* **Avon:** "Our vision: To be the company that best understands and satisfies the product, service and self-fulfillment needs of women—globally."

* **Polo (Ralph Lauren):** "We have redefined the American style by providing quality products,

creating worlds, and inviting people to take part in our dreams."

✳ **McDonald's:** "To be the world's best quick service restaurant experience. Being the best means providing outstanding quality, service, cleanliness, and value, so that we make every customer in every restaurant smile."

✳ **Microsoft:** "Our Vision: A personal computer in every home running Microsoft [MSFT] software."

✳ **Westin Hotels:** "Year after year, Westin and its people will be regarded as the best and most sought-after hotel and resort management group in North America."

✳ **Nike:** "To help Nike, Inc., and its consumers thrive in a sustainable economy where people, profit and planet are in balance."

✳ **Google:** "To organize the world's information and make it universally accessible and useful."

Mentoring takes on similar qualities to those vision statements it identifies what the process hopes to accomplish, it inspires, it focuses on being the best, and it assumes the potential exists to implement the vision.

Risks do exist in striving for goals that are currently quite a bit out of reach. Failure to attain a goal—even if it is perceived as a "stretch" to attain—may negatively impact the protégé's self-esteem or engender frustration. Other potential risks exist, as well. Daniel Markovitz, in an article titled "The Folly of Stretch Goals" that he posted to the Harvard Business Review blog, documented the "side effects" of asking people to extend almost beyond their capabilities. "Stretch goals can be terribly demotivating, overwhelming and unattainable," he wrote. Stretch goals sap employees' intrinsic motivation (which we discussed in Powerful Practice #2), says Markovitz. The enormity of the problem causes people to freeze up, and the extrinsic motivator of money crowds out the intrinsic motivators of learning and growth. Markovitz also cites Karl Weick's classic article, "Small Wins," which advocates recasting larger problems into smaller, tractable challenges that produce visible results (Markovitz 2012).

However, stretch goals are achieved through a series of small wins! That is how mentors help a protégé—by recommending a lofty ambition but then providing a pathway to its achievement.

Markovitz raises the issue of whether stretch goals foster unethical behavior, the notion being that lofty goals may engender cheating, cutting corners, exploiting customers, or otherwise promoting behaviors the individual would not otherwise even consider in the absence of documented stretch goals. Perhaps Markovitz is on to something about stretch goals: they should not be framed in a financial context, such as high compensation, excessive sales quotas, or company profit. The goals should be about *excellence*, just as the vision statements convey. For mentors, the identification and pursuit of stretch goals should focus on how the protégé can achieve superior levels of personal and professional excellence in performing his duties, and the non-monetary rewards that stem from such excellent performance.

But mentors do not approach the identification of stretch goals as increasing the protégé's opportunities to fail. For mentors, stretch goals are put in place to inspire extraordinary results. Mentors need to see beyond the obvious in the here and

now, and consider the virtually limitless future of their protégés to create achievements that would not have even been considered possible without the mentor–protégé relationship being
in place. Such is the fundamental value of the mentoring role.

Stretch goals are highly individualized. What might be
easy advancement for one could be a stretch for another. It
depends on their respective prior experience level, native skills,
academic background, leadership potential, and motivation
levels.

Case example: An individual has been an analyst for a
government contractor for three years on a project with 28
staff. He approaches a mentor about taking the career step of
becoming a team leader—after participating in many teams, it
seems like a logical step to advance valuable project skills. The
mentor challenges the protégé's assumptions about this incremental career growth objective. "What if instead of becoming a team leader," she asks, "we focus on what it would take
for you to become the overall project manager for the entire
team, with full accountability for execution of all tasks on the
contract?"

The protégé smiles. "I often wondered if I could do the PM
role. How would I prepare for it?" The stage is set for a discussion of a bona fide stretch goal. Even if the protégé indicates
that he had considered the prospect of project leadership, the
process of reviewing what it would take to achieve this outcome can reveal much about the protégé's career perspectives.
But more importantly, the mentor has raised the bar, and fa-
cilitated a search for fulfillment that stretches the protégé's potential. This is an essential aspect of mentoring: engendering
significant leaps to far higher levels of aspiration. Uncovering

and supporting stretch goals is integral to making mentoring as valuable as it can be.

The reasons why the analyst in our example may deem project leadership an unreachable goal are likely to sound rational, but the discussion invites an exploration of why this limit-setting cognition exists. One of the defining characteristics of a stretch goal is that, while exciting to contemplate, it seems difficult or almost impossible to achieve. For the goal to be a stretch, it should create a deliberate mismatch between the protégé's aspirations and ambitions and his or her present knowledge, skill set, and resources. To achieve the stretch goal, protégés need to learn to get more out of what they have.

How to best gauge if a goal represents a "stretch" for a protégé? The assessment can begin by eliciting the protégé's own perceptions of what would fulfill his or her professional aspirations. Such a discussion needs to be framed in optimism:

"Without considering the obstacles or reasons why it may be unrealistic, let's give you full reign over fulfilling your professional future. What would you be doing professionally five years and 10 years from now, if you had full control to make it happen?"

In listening to and assessing the protégé's response, and considering the limitations of the goals that the protégé has presented, the mentor is in a position to integrate the concept of stretch goals into the discussion. The concept allows the mind permission to explore a different future and new avenues to achieve this future. Importantly for mentors, setting stretch goals forces protégés to throw out processes they were applying before and look at their future from an entirely new perspective—a future that extends the presumed boundaries of protégés' potential.

If stretch goals engender purposefully wide-open exploration of protégés' full potential, and represent significant leaps from current reality, how do mentors assist beyond simply identifying them? While supporting the visioning skills of protégés to drive the process of establishing stretch goals, mentors also need to have methods that maintain the momentum built during the exploratory process. It is therefore important to develop a sound implementation plan. The planning process includes backing up from the goal to identify logical incremental interim milestones that create a sound pathway to goal attainment. But throughout the activities taken along the stretch goal pathway, mentors need to continue to provide additional support to the emotional component of process. That is, they need to reinforce the inspiration that helped craft the stretch goal in the first place.

Stretch goal milestones are important for both the protégé and mentor to understand, but they should not be too granular. They can be focused on major skill performance development stages, or be temporal, or both. That is, they can identify the incremental competencies needed to approach the stretch goal (as opposed to listing every daily activity taken to achieve the next competency level), or call for reviews of goal attainment at certain time intervals (for example, annually, as opposed to weekly), or they can combine the two. If the protégé has his or her own idea of a clearly laid-out plan to stretch goal attainment, the mentor's role is more to implement a schedule to review that the plan is being implemented effectively. If the protégé has no clearly understood path toward the stretch goal, then the mentor's role is to help create a logical sequence of achievements that foretell success in attaining the desired outcome.

The non-granularity of stretch-goal planning supports protégé autonomy during the process. Stretch goals are less useful for the protégé focused highly on extrinsic rewards and with little sense of an internal locus of control. These protégés simply do not possess the inspiration or motivation to go beyond their steady and reliable pathway to a more closed-ended future. Stretch goals are more for the intrinsically motivated protégé and/or the individual with a strong sense of an internal locus of control. With autonomy comes the power to determine the pathway to a stretch goal and the timing of its attainment. A mentor need not necessarily dictate the pace of stretch-goal attainment, but rather serve as a consistent sounding board and interpreter of how the protégé is progressing toward achieving these goals that align with attaining higher levels of self-actualization.

Should the mentor discuss a backup plan in case the stretch goal appears to be too far out of reach? Many experienced mentors think not—mentoring is more about the process of striving for excellence than supporting a protégé through his or her vulnerability to failure. The mentors we canvassed on this subject, to a person, all came back with their favorite quote or saying about endeavoring to attain stretch goals. Here is a list of those that easily rolled off seasoned mentors' lips. Our advice is to memorize one of these, or other applicable quotes that resonate the most with you, and share them with your protégé in the context of discussing his or her stretch goals and the inherent risks in establishing them.

✳ Reach for the sky, because if you should happen to miss, you'll still be among the stars. (Musician Les Brown)

✳ Far away, there in the sunshine, are my highest aspirations. I may not reach them, but I can look up and see their beauty, believe in them, and try to follow where they lead. (Louisa May Alcott)

✳ Life is too short to be small. (Benjamin Disraeli)

✳ We aim above the mark to hit the mark. (Ralph Waldo Emerson)

✳ You can't rest unless you set goals that make you stretch. (Author Tom Hopkins)

✳ Keep your eyes on the stars but keep your feet on the ground. (Theodore Roosevelt)

✳ As long as you're going to be thinking anyway, think BIG. (Donald Trump)

Lastly, in the brilliant mixed logic of Yogi Berra: You've got to be very careful if you don't know where you're going, because you might not get there.

Summary

Mentors are most valuable when they facilitate a process of potential-fulfillment that sets the bar for future self-actualization very high. The truth is that individuals tend to make steady, incremental advances in their career without mentoring support; thus, the mentor role is to provide the inspiration and cognitive prodding to accelerate potential development.

For the protégé who has identified a stretch goal and commits to attaining it, the mentor can support a mutual understanding of the pathway that makes the goal-attainment possible. To promote the autonomy of the more intrinsically motivated protégé, mentors can serve as a facilitator—this is their defining role, versus the coach or supervisor more prone to dictate the terms of a developmental process. Mentors are likely to ask, "So, how do we get there?" Posing this question creates opportunities for the mentor to add wisdom, experience, and counsel to the natural pathway to potential-fulfillment.

CHAPTER 10

Powerful Practice #5 of Really Great Mentors:

Reinforce the Importance of Safeguarding Credibility

If the role of mentoring is one that focuses on building character, expanding expertise, and placing a mirror in front of behaviors that are either admired or disappointing to others, then the concept of credibility is central to this support role. If the mentor achieves nothing except enhancing the credibility of the protégé, the results of such mentoring guidance will be extremely valuable.

Credibility is, in part, about the alignment of one's words and actions. Individuals with credibility are fully believable in the statements they make. The preeminent journalist of the mid-20th century, Edward R. Murrow, wrote that to be persuasive we must be believable; to be believable we must be credible; to be credible we must be truthful. Mentors must be mindful of this credibility mantra. Because persuasiveness is a desirable and even necessary attribute of those holding the types of higher-level positions to which protégés aspire, mentors need to take notice of what protégés say they will do, and then what they actually do.

Credibility issues may arise in mentoring discussions of how professional challenges were handled. Mentors need to confront any inconsistencies that are evident in the protégés' words and actions. Perhaps the issue involved promises made to others that the protégé now realizes will be difficult to keep. Perhaps a midstream course change occurred that caused the protégé to take a credibility-diminishing new direction, however sound the reason was for doing so. By highlighting longer-term implications of actions in such circumstances, mentors emphasize their commitment to behaviors that enhance rather than diminish personal and professional credibility. The message from mentor to protégé is simple: credibility is difficult to earn, but can be lost in a single misstep.

Credibility is also about alignment between professed values and subsequent behaviors. As mentor and protégé are becoming acquainted, it is important to spend time exploring and identifying each other's respective values. These discussions form the basis for understanding the beliefs that underlie behaviors shown by both mentor and protégé. A mentor can ask the protégé to develop and share a "Credo Statement" or "I believe..." sentences that reflect the protégé's values.

Another useful technique to gain shared understandings of protégés' values is to ask them to write an introductory speech to a future farewell dinner at which the protégé is the guest of honor. The speech should point out the values the protégé has exemplified, which is the primary reason why people wish to pay tribute to him or her. This exercise forces the protégé to consider the values that he or she would like to convey to others repeatedly and without exception, which garner admiration from others.

Another values-clarification exercise mentors can use with protégés is to explore a person in history whom the protégé greatly admires. Once this person is identified and the reasons for selecting this person are explored, the mentor can refer back to this choice in the future by asking, "What do you think [the most admired person] would have done in that circumstance?"

When individuals' beliefs, ideas or thoughts, and actions are in sync, credibility is enhanced. But this attribute is also about creating an impression among others that the individual's actions and decisions stem from a realistic, proven basis of expertise. Honesty is always a good policy, but it alone does not guarantee professional credibility. Others must trust that protégés have the proven technical capabilities and readiness to perform in the role they hold, or hope to hold.

If you examine the concept of technical credibility, you will learn that such credibility involves several key behaviors. These are the behaviors that mentors can support, role model, advocate, and help protégés work toward. The credible protégé...

* ✳ **Stays informed about the technical field, and applies such knowledge effectively.** Mentors can point to sources of increased knowledge to enhance technical credibility, and discuss how the protégé applies this knowledge to different work circumstances and challenges.

* ✳ **Uses good judgment to handle basic issues and problems.** Mentors use their time wisely by

focusing on the protégé's difficult judgment calls. These decisions typically have multiple potential options from which to choose, each with its own implications downstream. Mentoring is a highly effective process for protégés who seek the wisdom and seasoned guidance of an individual who has had to address relevant or highly similar circumstances in their professional lives.

❋ **Tracks new advances and cutting-edge developments in the technical field.** To be credible, one must be current about what is occurring in one's field. Mentors may not have all the information a protégé needs to remain current, but they need to have good ideas about where the protégé can go to learn what he or she needs to learn to be on the cutting edge of best practices and thought leadership. Mentors, in essence, are stewards of credibility-enhancing knowledge management for their protégés.

❋ **Modifies and creates new methods and techniques in response to changing technology.** Here, professional credibility is tied to the protégé's ability to demonstrate innovation and attention-gathering creativity. Mentors are champions of their protégés' innovation, because they know the inventors of the world create a special place for themselves among those without the interest or capabilities to discover new and better ways of doing things. In almost all the famous mentor–protégé pairing through history, the result of these relationships was discovery, thought leadership, and, consequently, almost instant or highly enhanced personal and/or professional credibility.

Mentors can confirm and further explore these aspects of technical credibility by focusing on models they have witnessed in their careers. They can say:

※ "Tell me about what behaviors and skills are shown by those in your field whom others trust as credible and capable professionals."

※ "How did these professionals earn their professional credibility?"

The responses from protégés are likely to trend toward the following:

※ **Applicable knowledge.** What professionals know about the field in which they practice makes them credible as a source of information. This is especially pertinent when questions or issues are raised that include an element of complexity.

※ **Relevant work experience.** The functions and positions the professional has held during his or her career bring credibility, because they demonstrate a history of performance in roles where certain expertise and competencies were required.

※ **Personal or academic background.** Schools the professional attended can enhance credibility, especially if these institutions have a superior reputation in the field (for example, specialized graduate schools) or that show a track record of academic accomplishment (for example, Ivy League or top-20 schools).

✳ **Pertinent professional credentials.**
   Certifications the professional holds demonstrate
   to peers that he or she possesses core and/or advanced competencies within the profession.

The driver behind maintaining one's technical capability is
the requirement that a credible professional knows what he or
she is talking about. Others gauge whether an individual tends
to communicate from a position of authority about an issue,
or if he tends to overestimate his own fund of knowledge. It is
important that the mentor convey the message that knowledge
is power, and that one should be more of a listener or inquirer
if information is not known (rather than trying to appear as if
the information is known).

Developing a sound, logical career path enhances opportunities that the protégé will be credible within each new role to
which she advances. Mentors can also sponsor protégés for new
and more challenging work experiences, or guide them about
how they could qualify to do far more in their professional careers than they are doing now.

Whereas protégés' prior academic backgrounds are often a
fait accompli for mentors, guidance toward professional courses
or new training programs can add to the protégés' professional
credibility. Similarly, mentors can advocate that protégés make
the effort to achieve professional certifications that demonstrate prerequisite competencies or show evidence of relevant
competencies at the level required by a position. In an earlier
example we discussed an analyst who might take on a stretch
goal of becoming a project manager. The plan to reach this
goal would probably include attaining certification as a Project
Management Professional (PMP).

To enhance and advocate for safeguarding professional credibility, **mentors must reinforce to their protégés several guiding principles:**

※ **Do what you say you will do.** Insist that protégés align their behaviors and actions with their words.

※ **Don't make promises you can't keep.** The message is to under-promise and over-deliver.

※ **Remain honest and forthright even when the truth hurts.** Being a straight-shooter is admirable because it demonstrates the overarching value of safeguarding one's credibility.

※ **Frequently review relevant lessons learned.** This activity helps professionals share credible past experiences when similar problems were faced, and what lessons were learned that support sound methodologies to be used in the future.

※ **Integrate the values announced by the organization with your own.** Organizations' vision statements and professed values set implicit behavioral expectations that the protégé should integrate into everyday professional practice. Doing so gets protégés noticed and advances career opportunities.

※ **Align training plans with efforts to enhance credibility.** Identify the gaps in learning that provide obstacles to gaining the confidence and trust of those who have a say in determining the protégé's future.

※ **Enhance your professional knowledge on a continuous basis—stay on the leading edge.** Professional dinosaurs (even those who are relatively young) lose their credibility very rapidly.

※ **Seek to be perceived as an innovator.** Discoverers and creators of new processes and "better mouse traps" receive significant recognition for their new ideas—and the credibility that accompanies such recognition.

Summary

The context of effective mentoring lies in guiding a protégé to greater levels of professional credibility. The methods mentors apply to enhancing their protégés' credibility involve four major factors:

1. **Alignment of words and actions.** Mentors point out the credibility link between one's communications, vocal or written, and one's actions. It is best to emphasize a credibility framework that under-promises and over-delivers.

2. **Alignment of professed values and behaviors.** If a manager states his "door is always open" as evidence of the value he places on full and unobstructed communication with others, and yet the door to his office is closed most of the day, others will come to doubt the manager's credibility. Uncover the protégés' abiding beliefs and values, and discuss any personal or professional behaviors that best reflect or might not reflect these values.

3. **Alignment of organizational values and individual values.** Organizations often espouse certain values, such as "people before processes," transparency of information, and promoting from within whenever possible. When individual values are not fully aligned with organizational values, it is inevitable that the misalignment will engender credibility issues. Mentors must reinforce an understanding both of organizational values and of values that protégés portray through certain behaviors, to address any inconsistencies between what the organization expects and what protégés do in practice.

4. **Advancement of technical knowledge and skills.** Protégés' gain respect and enhance advancement opportunities when they are deemed by others and knowledgeable, innovative, credentialed, and up-to-date on their respective professional fields.

CHAPTER 11

Powerful Practice #6 of Really Great Mentors:

Foster Strategic Thinking

Thus far, our recommendations have focused on a range of behavioral aspects for performing in the mentoring role: modeling ways to relate with others, understanding underlying motivations, inspiring by escalating aspirations, and developing means to build a sound professional reputation. Yet, the mentor role can also serve as a teacher of desirable thinking skills. When performing at lower professional levels, one might be able to get by with letting others do the thinking, and focusing more on implementing the direction these senior managers advocate. But protégés make best use of a mentor when they aspire to more than a following role. They are likely to seek opportunities to be the ones thinking through solutions and developing strategies that align with organizational objectives.

When performed at an advanced level, strategic thinking facilitates deeper, more holistic, and more accurate interpretations of complex or even conflicting data. Strategic thinking increases the probability of a desirable outcome. Strategic thinking is purposeful, reasoned, and goal-directed. It is the kind of thinking involved in solving problems. Mentors often must transform protégés more accustomed to being observers or reactive to events around them into strategic thinkers who demonstrate the capability to filter through the meaning of diverse sets of information.

Strategic thinking uncovers interpretations and abstract, generalized meanings from complex information. Indeed, it is a skill of coping with or even thriving in an environment of complexity. Few, if any, strategic decisions are clear-cut or without some adverse consequences. Strategic thinking skills are valuable because complexity is inevitable, and because those who can separate the drivers of future direction from factors that are irrelevant from a longer-term perspective are of great benefit to any organization.

The converse assumption, that toxic or insufficient thinking undermines the development of effective strategies, is just as pertinent. By "toxic thinking," we mean cognitions that filter information through a lens of negativity, pessimism, and reasons why certain options will never work. Strategic thinkers not only convey the emotionally intelligent trait of optimism, but they also have an unending hunger to reason through the data to which they have access, knowing that this information invariably provides clues to uncovering the most potent strategic plan.

Protégés' value to the organization is influenced largely by how well they separate themselves from individuals who neither own nor wish to develop strategic thinking skills. When protégés make the leap from being followers to being strategists, they demonstrate their readiness to move beyond the more obvious path to one characterized by thoughtfulness and value-adding insight. But the leap often requires a significant paradigm shift. Mentors are in an ideal position to support a process that encourages a more strategic manner of thinking through challenges. The skill being taught is less a function of native intelligence and more a function of wiring the brain to reason through alternatives and select the soundest strategic direction.

Research on developing the ability to think more strategically focuses on three cognitive "platforms" from which the desired thinking behaviors stem:

1. Strategic attention
2. Integrated reasoning/data interpretation
3. Advocating for strategic innovation

Let's review each of these and how mentors can facilitate the learning of competencies that support the objectives of each of these strategic thinking platforms.

1. Strategic Attention

As Arthur Miller wrote about his character Willy Loman in *Death of a Salesman*, "attention must be paid." Strategic attention to useful information is an awareness skill. That is, protégés may raise issues for discussion with their mentors that focus more on their here-and-now issues, while forsaking considerations of a longer-term and more strategic nature. But thinking more strategically means paying attention to the strategic intents of those involved in a circumstance. Strategic intent provides the focus that allows individuals to marshal and leverage their energy, to focus attention, to resist distraction, and to concentrate for as long as it takes to achieve a goal.

Mentors can respond to questions about here-and-now issues by shifting the attention to their strategic implications:

"What do you think all this means, from a longer-term perspective? Why have the current circumstances occurred, and what are the trends to anticipate for the future? I think it is more important to pay attention to that."

Effective mentoring forces the protégé to get beyond the immediate challenges and pay greater attention to future implications of current challenges. "Finger in the dike" solutions are of far less value in a mentoring context than those that engender a more strategic, lasting solution.

When considering future strategies for a division or an overall organization, the strategically minded individual must pay attention to the most useful internal and external information sources that inform future strategy. Consequently, the strategic thinker must be proactive about the means to collect data and interact with others about the most relevant data. Mentors need to draw their protégés' attention toward the ongoing imperative to address the following questions:

"What information is important for you to assemble, to develop a basis for influencing your thinking about the correct and most pertinent strategy going forward? And how will you collect this information?"

Mentors by definition tend to be more experienced than their protégés about such valuable information sources and methods to gain access to them. This is mentoring in the teaching and advisory role. Applying their experience in performing their own strategic thinking, mentors advise protégés about the availability of useful data and how to go about aggregating it. Information to be collected commonly exists in two primary spheres: internal (within the organization, collected as a matter of course by management control processes) and external (range of industry forums and networking, industry experts, pertinent periodicals/journals, news and social media, government-collected and published data, and other sources unique to a specific industry).

Mentors can also advise protégés about which information offers the most value or benefit with respect to the strategic issue being considered, from the mentors' prior experience. You might have found data source #1 to be extremely valuable and data source #2 to be largely useless. Mentors add value by providing guidance about ways to streamline the information to be gathered and by pointing protégés toward the data that requires the most attention.

Typically, internal sources of information are accessible through various management or quality-control activities at the organization. For example, when organizations set various goals (for example, on-budget performance, revenue growth, market share, profit/margin, number of employees, new product development, and so on), they will establish measurement systems to assess whether these goals are being met. The metrics that enable such an assessment of goal attainment are usually collected on a routine basis, as are variances against preset standards or assumptions based on actual performance measurements.

Mentors can assist their protégés in determining if the data being collected to inform future strategy is sufficient, and well-targeted. Perhaps management control systems are gathering information for use as a diagnostic tool for current performance assessments, but other information would be more valuable as a benchmark from which to base future strategies or direction. Paying proactive attention to the information on which to base strategies is an important initial form of value-added strategic thinking. Knowledge enables strategy, so powerful strategies depend largely on the utility of the information from which the strategic decisions were made. Effective mentors advise protégés about the best knowledge-enhancing methodologies.

Mentors also apply their experience to valuable networks and information sources external to the organization. They may share examples of how they enhanced their own learning about an issue through tapping a specific external source of information. Mentors may sponsor a protégé within an industry association or network to enable him or her to have greater access to those who can provide useful information.

2. Integrated Reasoning/ Data Interpretation

Once information is gathered and attended to, the protégé then must have the skill to reason through and develop interpretations of the data. Mentors are in a unique position to facilitate the development of their protégés' critical thinking skills. Mentors need to prod protégés to process information differently than they might have before. The process that mentors advocate is about generating interpretations, themes, or general trends from existing information. Rather than focusing on simply retaining facts, strategic thinking focuses on uncovering the underlying meaning of what has occurred.

Mentors can teach more critical and strategic thinking by reinforcing the value of performing various steps that support integrated reasoning and sound interpretations of data. These steps include:

※ **Analyzing the issue** by breaking overall circumstances into smaller parts to uncover their true nature. For example, if the issue is customer complaints about a product or service, the best way to interpret what is going on is to look at the various process steps that contribute to the circumstances that customers are complaining about.

※ **Applying standards.** Interpretations require some grounding in what are generally acceptable standards, from which to make comparisons. For example, if a physician is mentoring a more junior physician about a clinical dilemma, the well-established medial pathway from symptom presentation to treatment determination serves as a touchstone in making interpretations about the presenting clinical data.

※ **Discriminating differences and similarities.** Mentors can advise about ways to group or rank different factors or variables, to enable the reasoning or interpretation activity. This strategic thinking skill is of particular importance when the issue under consideration is highly complex. Without performing the grouping effort, the critical thinker is unable to simplify the process of uncovering meanings behind a vast array of data.

✳ **Performing additional information seeking.** At times, the information gathered up to the point of making strategic determinations has provided direction to the thinking process but is insufficient to make final strategic decisions. More information of a targeted nature might be needed. Strategic thinkers uncover what they need to know to formulate a valid strategy, and develop a means to gather this additional information.

✳ **Conducting logical reasoning.** Mentors can guide protégés about how to draw inferences effectively or how to develop interpretations justified by the available information. They can challenge flawed reasoning as well, pointing out the missing pieces or errors in inferring C from evidence A combined with evidence B.

✳ **Predicting future behavior.** Strategy is all about predicting the future. Mentors can advise about formulating a strategic plan by helping to anticipate the consequences of implementing the plan, and by uncovering risks that might need to be identified and potentially mitigated once the plan is underway.

✳ **Transforming complex knowledge into a singular vision.** Strategies are by nature simplified activities amid complex circumstances. There is little value in developing strategies that are too complex to implement. Mentors can assist in simplifying a developing strategy when protégés are stuck on thinking about a far too complicated direction to take.

3. Advocating for Strategic Innovation

Critical thinking yields new insights about the meaning of available data. Consequently, the process is likely to elicit new understandings that promote creativity and innovation. Strategic thinking challenges the status quo, and identifies better, more efficient, and more effective ways of accomplishing the same desired outcomes. The skill of strategic thinking adds value to an organization when it engenders new insights that guide the right resources in a new and better direction. Mentors prod protégés to think beyond the obvious and customary, with the message that transformational thinking, while posing some risks, offers tremendous upside rewards—including the credibility discussed in the previous Powerful Practice—when the innovative strategies protégés developed and advocated are eventually proven true.

The Mentor as a Role Model for Strategic Thinking Competencies

The mentor is in a unique position to role-model strategic thinking, because mentoring discussions are often about what the future holds and the alternatives that must be considered. Three techniques are highly valuable to exhibit for protégés, as the two of you work through various issues involving career or business strategy:

1. Asking the most penetrating questions
2. Reframing and simplifying issues to enable a review of alternatives
3. Considering alternative assumptions

1. Asking the Most Penetrating Questions

By "penetrating questions," we mean those that drill down deeper, that assume the two of you share information of a more superficial nature or on a surface level, but do not share a mutual understanding as yet about certain aspects of causality or true precipitating circumstances. Some mentors tell us that their line of questioning tends to follow the need to discover the true intent of the protégé and of the various protagonists in the protégé's circumstances. "What does so-and-so really want at the end of this decision-making process? What are this person's core motives?" Another method of questioning is the Six Sigma method of analyzing the root causes of problems. It involves "the Five Whys." To use this method, **Step 1** is to write a stated problem that the protégé is experiencing as best you can frame it. Writing down the issue for both mentor and protégé to see helps the two of you normalize the problem and describe it completely. It also helps the two of you focus on the same problem. Then, for **Step 2**, ask *why* the problem happens, and write the answer down below the problem. If the answer you just provided does not identify the root cause of the problem you wrote down in Step 1, **Step 3** is to ask *why* again and write that answer down. Loop back to Step 3 until the two of you are in agreement that the problem's root cause has been identified. This effort may take fewer or more than five *whys*. But five *whys* is the usual or modal amount of questions needed to penetrate deeper and bring you closer to the causes that inform the best strategies.

2. Reframing and Simplifying Issues to Enable a Review of Alternatives and Adjustment to Them

Strategies are the most impactful when they are characterized by simplicity. Complexity mitigates both the understanding and the application of effective strategies. Understanding this, mentors can model efforts to reframe the many variables into a common and more straightforward understanding. Often, a mentor will reframe and simplify issues by reverting the exploration back to the protégé's expressed goals, including the stretch goals we discussed in Powerful Practice #4. Strategies need clearly identified goals, and if that work has already been done (goal clarification), then most issues can be reframed against the desired outcomes to which the two of you have agreed.

3. Considering Alternative Assumptions

Maintaining the status quo is not really a strategy. It is a decision, but it forsakes the value of strategic thinking. However, actively considering alternative assumptions elicits the taking of new directions toward a potential strategy or solution to attain a desired outcome.

Case example: A protégé is fretting over the potential loss of a big account because the client has asked for an open competition among potential vendors for the work to start on January 1 of the following year. The protégé's sense is that the client is getting substantial financial pressure from his superiors to cut costs, and he sees the decision to open up the work to a competitive procurement of the next contract as a way to potentially save money while getting the same level of service.

Therefore, the protégé is focused on getting to the right price point to maintain the business. Perhaps the client will pay a slight premium to retain the incumbent team, but not much of one, in the protégé's view. The mentor takes a different tack than questioning about ways to build the price to win the business. The mentor asks, "Tell me, what keeps this client awake at night? What are his hot buttons?" The mentor then goes on to ask about different non-monetary ways to maintain a relationship with the client that would cause the client to deem any change in vendors as too risky, imprudent, and short-sighted. "What would make this client shine to his superiors? What services can you provide or have you provided that are indispensable to him? Mentors can complete this line of strategic questioning by advocating the following credo: "Always add value before lowering price."

Summary

Mentoring is most valuable when it is performed in the context of facilitating thought leadership instead of thought-following behaviors. Thought leadership is a function of finding meaning within complex sets of information, which must be filtered to enable sound interpretations of the data. Mentors direct protégés to be more attentive to longer-term strategy and meaning behind events. The skill of strategic thinking is a disciplined process characterized by methods to analyze, differentiate, and synthesize disparate pieces of information. The highest value elicited from developing strategic thinking skills occurs when the process yields innovation and creativity, or paradigm shifts away from more stale approaches to addressing future requirements.

CHAPTER 12

———◆———

*Powerful Practice #7 of
Really Great Mentors:*

**Encourage the Protégé to
Draft an Initial Mentoring
Plan, on His or Her Own**

Even the most intrinsically motivated protégés can benefit from collaborating on and documenting a plan that outlines an approach to developing their potential, both in the near term and the long term. Mentoring Plans provide a touchstone for measuring the desired outcomes to which the protégé and mentor have agreed. The Mentoring Plan is less about providing rigid structure to the mentoring process and more about reinforcing a shared vision among protégé and mentor about what the relationship hopes to accomplish and the methods for attaining these goals. It is a collaboration tool, enabling rather than restricting broad-based discussions of protégés' future interests and pathways to optimizing their potential.

In organizationally sponsored mentoring programs, developing Mentoring Plans may be required and viewed more as a duty than as a value-adding tool. But mentors and protégés need to recognize that they are involved in a relationship that develops a plan, whether documented or not. Mentoring is not simply a verbal exchange between a more senior professional with a more junior professional. Mentoring is results-oriented. Plans that document these desired results allow protégés to confirm the direction to which they hope to head.

Developing a Mentoring Plan is more about the process of collaboration than the document itself. The plan is a facilitator for discussions about how to get from the present to a more desired future. It creates a spirit of accountability, by documenting the protégé's responsibilities in making that desired future happen. Adaptable to new circumstances, the Mentoring Plan keeps a record of what has emerged as a result of the process of collaboration between mentor and protégé in their relationship. Without a plan, mentors and protégés may find that they lose track of the decisions they have made together and the discussions that led to these decisions. Plans enable the mentor and protégé to revisit the content of their prior interactions, especially those that reviewed goals upon which the relationship is focusing. When a substantial agreement is reached during the mentoring process, the mentor can note, "That belongs in our plan!" The plan confirms that the issue being reviewed requires follow-up and subsequent additional review.

To elicit ideas for the mentoring that will take place, mentors can assign protégés the task of developing an initial draft of the Mentoring Plan. Doing so enables protégés to take the time to reflect on and carefully craft their personal vision statement relating to receiving mentoring, and to cite some ideas they have about interim goals to achieve.

Protégés can develop their Mentoring Plan draft by using the following step-by-step approach.

Step 1: Conduct a Self-Assessment

※ Assess their skills, strengths, and areas that need development.

※ Take a realistic look at their current abilities. If at all possible participate in multi-rater feedback surveys, or simply ask your boss, peers, teachers, coaches, counselors, family, and/or friends to rate you on various important skills and attributes (for example, interpersonal aptitudes, job knowledge, respect for others, follow-up/responsiveness, and so on).

※ Outline their long-term objectives. Ask themselves a) What type of work would they like to be doing? b) Where would they like to be in this organization? c) What is important to them in a career?

Step 2: Survey Opportunities

※ Identify career and personal opportunities and select from those that interest them.

※ Identify developmental needs by comparing current skills and strengths with those needed for their career choice.

※ Prioritize their developmental areas to prepare for discussions about how these should be addressed with a mentor.

Step 3: Write Down a Mentoring Plan for Themselves

A Mentoring Plan maps out a general path and helps match skills/strengths to career choices. Note that the Mentoring Plan is likely to be a changing document; needs and goals will almost certainly evolve over time. The aim is for the protégé to identify areas for development and provide a way to address each of these areas. To develop this Mentoring Plan:

※ Identify an area for development, from the list developed in Step 2.

※ Identify an objective tied to that area for development (protégés can separate personal from professional areas they wish to develop).

※ Identify activities that would support achievement of the objective tied to the self-identified area of development.

※ Identify a milestone toward attainment of the objective tied to the self-identified area of development, and a time for review of the progress made.

※ Identify learning needs or knowledge gaps needed to attain the milestones, and methods to address these needs or close the knowledge gap.

Consequently, the plan can be laid out as a matrix of **Areas for Development**, **Activities and Methods** used to perform them, the **Frequency** of activity performance, and **Desired Learning Outcomes**, as expressed by interim milestones toward goal attainment. Finally, the plan should include responsibility assignments (for example, **To Be Completed By** and **Review Dates**). This data facilitates timing when shared assessments of activity performance will occur, and the extent to which objectives are being met. If the protégé wishes the plan to document activities that the mentor will perform, such as reaching out to an external resource regarding a sponsorship opportunity, an additional **Person Responsible** column is valuable to include. Finally, the plan should have a **Lifelong Learning** section. We discuss the components of this section of the plan in Powerful Practice #9.

Step 4: Discuss the Mentoring Plan When It Is Ready for Mutual Review

The discussion of the protégé-developed draft Mentoring Plan may occur across multiple sessions, with an extended examination of the information the protégé presents in the plan. When the protégé produces this initial plan draft, the mentor should take time alone reviewing it to gain insights into the protégé's approach to the mentoring process. The plan draft can provide information about the intrinsic and extrinsic motivations of the protégé, and if the vision statement aligns with identified objectives. After performing this review offline (in other words, not in the midst of a mentoring session), the mentor can begin subsequent interaction with the protégé by probing with questions that seek to better understand the plan's contents and the direction for mentoring that it implies. Ultimately, the draft plan as revised becomes the official Mentoring Plan that guides the direction of future learning within the mentor-protégé relationship. Then, mentor and protégé should develop a vocal or written contract to apply their efforts to the issues, challenges, and priorities documented in the Mentoring Plan.

Step 5: Revise and Modify the Plan as Necessary

The Mentoring Plan is never cast in stone, and needs to be modified as circumstances and goals change. The challenge is to be flexible and open to change. Furthermore, Mentoring Plans need not be too granular or highly itemized. It is not the plan's intention to provide hour-by-hour or day-to-day direction on activities to develop potential in the protégé. Mentoring Plans are more "big picture"-oriented. They document substantial goals and major milestones on the path to achieving objectives. Ideally, the plan is not an onerous or overly complicated document to complete. It needs to be right-sized to match its purpose: providing a means to collaborate on understanding the purpose of the mentor–protégé relationship, documenting a shared vision of the direction to take in achieving what the protégé hopes to achieve, and creating accountability to stay on course.

How does the Mentoring Plan advocate for and motivate excellence? Earlier, we discussed the concept of vision statements in the context of developing stretch goals. The Mentoring Plan should include a **vision statement**, confirming the shared understanding of the answer to the question, "Why are we here?" Again, vision statements identify what the mentoring process hopes to accomplish. They should be inspirational, focusing on the protégé being the best he or she can be, and they assume the potential exists to transform the vision into an achievable future.

Similar to other types of planning processes, the Mentoring Plan follows a cyclical path from *assessment* to *plan development* to *execution* to *reviewing results*. There is no point in developing a Mentoring Plan if it lies on a shelf or in digital folder, without impacting the mentoring process at all. It should be accessible and visible, and an indirect component of each mentoring interaction.

The plan should be updated as needed, especially when mentor and protégé decide on the value of new activities or outcomes, or of taking a substantially new direction in the relationship. Outdated Mentoring Plans mean that they are not truly part of the mentoring process. Keeping the plan current is a role that mentors and protégés should share, given the inherently collaborative nature of the planning process.

Summary

The process need not be bogged down in extensive administrivia, but mentoring does require planning and well-understood accountability for implementing decisions made in the relationship. The Mentoring Plan is a tool to enhance mentor–protégé collaboration, beginning with coming to a shared understanding of the protégé's vision of his or her future. Planning offers a means to uncover the motivations that drive the protégé's interest in learning new things. The Mentoring Plan plays an integral role in providing value-added organization to efforts focused on developing the protégé's full potential.

It is useful to assign protégés with the responsibility of drafting an initial Mentoring Plan. This method reinforces that the plan is really about the protégé and his or her aspirations. It also sets the tone from the beginning of the relationship that the mentoring process is guided by what the protégé hopes to accomplish. Just as mentoring is an other-oriented activity, mentoring planning needs to be based on the protégé's fundamental objectives and vision for what will take place in the relationship.

CHAPTER 13

———◆———

Powerful Practice #8 of
Really Great Mentors:

Identify and Leverage
Teachable Moments

A teachable moment occurs at the point in time when learning a specific topic or idea becomes possible or easiest. The concept was popularized by Robert Havighurst in his 1952 book *Human Development and Education*. In the context of theories of enhancing learning, Havighurst explained, "A developmental task is a task which is learned at a specific point and which makes achievement of succeeding tasks possible. When the timing is right, the ability to learn a particular task will be possible. This is referred to as a 'teachable moment.' It is important to keep in mind that unless the time is right, learning will not occur. Hence, it is important to repeat important points whenever possible so that when a student's teachable moment occurs, s/he can benefit from the knowledge" (Havighurst 1953).

The phrase sometimes denotes not a developmental stage, but rather that moment when a unique, high-interest situation arises that lends itself to discussion of a particular topic. The teachable moment is the narrow window of opportunity to show a protégé how a circumstance represents an opportunity to achieve a goal established in the Mentoring Plan. Parents often use this concept when their children encounter difficulties, have questions, and are eager to listen to advice about specific situations. Healthcare givers use this concept to address a needed behavioral change, such as smoking cessation, weight loss, or dietary changes. When your doctor brings out a chest X-ray showing black spots caused by lengthy smoking, it can shake you out of a lackadaisical attitude about the harmfulness of smoking—this is a teaching moment. When a mentor identifies an instance when the protégé is demonstrating behaviors counter to his or her objectives, and it has caused some type of repercussion on the job, it can be valuable to use this moment to reinforce some key concepts that have anchored the mentor's ongoing advisory and guidance approach.

Finding a teachable moment necessitates the mentor's personal engagement with the protégé's issues and problems. The Latin phrase *in vivo* implies living in the moment—literally, "in life"—and it applies to identifying when a life moment demonstrates a truth or a reality. Mentors sometimes approach protégé issues retrospectively, allowing time to provide perspective and potentially additional information about an issue, but this Powerful Practice of Really Great Mentors brings forward the powerful impact of here-and-now interventions, when an opportunity is available to reinforce a learning objective. Waiting for a different moment won't do—the teachable moment is one that must be taken advantage of *now!*

For mentors, the ideal teachable moment is important to recognize. It is a moment when the issue under consideration within the mentor–protégé relationship fully aligns with circumstances that can be used to illuminate the best course of action or intervention. Mentors will need to build an intuitive appreciation of the anticipated moment when teaching a skill or addressing a development issue might be strongest. This requires an understanding of their protégé's consciousness; that is, what he or she is thinking and feeling at a given point in time.

Some researchers call this a point of synchronicity. What is in sync in this case is an event or circumstance and the protégé's cognitive and affective response to the event or circumstance. The intervention that might leverage the prior two components already in alignment creates synchronicity. When such synchronicity occurs, the mentor can be presented with a teachable moment of intense, insightful, and meaningful learning experience that was not planned but suddenly just happened. Mentors intuitive enough to recognize the phenomenon and conscious of its potential significance can use the moment to emphasize how the event represents exactly what the mentor and protégé have discussed before.

Let's consider some examples, drawn from the powerful practices of mentoring we have already presented.

Taking advantage of a teachable moment to reinforce the value of emotionally intelligent self-management:

> *A protégé arrives at a mentoring session in a state of high anxiety. The protégé's boss has just informed the team that the deadline for producing a report needs to be changed, due to new customer demands—he needs the*

report in three days rather than two weeks, which was the deadline that had originally been set. The protégé is visibly shaken and unable to even think through a plan to produce the report by this new aggressive deadline. The mentor listens and observes the situation and circumstances, and suddenly rises out his chair and suggests, "Let's go for a walk. I find that a bit of fresh air and exercise is a good way to clear the mind." "Now?" the protégé asks. "I don't have a lot of extra time right now."

"Yes, now. Let's go," the mentor insists. So they leave the office, take a walk outside, and discuss other things besides the looming deadline, such as their respective plans for the upcoming Mother's Day. Thirty minutes later, when they return to the office, the mentor asks the protégé if he is in a better state of mind to consider how to meet the boss's new report deadline. The protégé responds, "Yes, let's think through some ideas."

The skill being taught is applying emotionally intelligent self-management skills to trying circumstances. The teachable moment came when a particularly trying circumstance occurred, and the learner was responding in a manner that offered a sound example of behavior that was detrimental to uncovering a solution to the problem with a clear mind. The mentor took the unorthodox approach of recommending his own self-management method of coping with stress through disengaging from the circumstances for a short period of time. The mentor modeled how taking a relaxing break with a bit of exercise when stress levels are inordinately high can provide the emotional relaxation to return to the fray with more emotional calmness and insight.

Taking advantage of a teachable moment to reinforce the value of uncovering intrinsic and extrinsic motivation:

A protégé insists time and again to the mentor that she considers professional advancement as alluring only in the context of making more money. The protégé espouses the premise that learning new skills is fine, but only toward the objective of making additional income—otherwise the skill is of little use to her. A Mentoring Plan is established with certain milestones set for developing new knowledge and skills incrementally, aligned with the professional advancement that includes higher compensation. At a point when a review was due about whether certain milestones had been attained, the protégé enters the mentoring session with a large smile on her face, and excitement in her voice. She had met her objective, and she explains all the positive ramifications of doing so—none of which involve financial gains. Instead, the positive ramifications have to do with recognition of her achievements by others, greater self-esteem, and the view that she would like to continue on the path toward greater development of her potential. The mentor provides feedback to the protégé about how it seems she is gaining a greater appreciation for processes that bring her enjoyment and a sense of accomplishment, due to her own efforts. "I haven't heard a word about the impact these accomplishments have on your earning power," the mentor says. "Perhaps you are motivated to achieve greater skills by more than the prospect of a bigger paycheck, after all." The protégé nods her head in agreement. "I'm just really happy knowing I can reach the goal that we set."

The teaching moment occurred when a purportedly extrinsically motivated individual demonstrated the more valuable intrinsic motivation to learn how to perform a certain skill. The mentor noted with a gentle reminder that the protégé had shown little prior interest in developing any skill that would not lead rather directly to more income, and that it now appeared she was able to recognize the value and importance of efforts to achieve outcomes that stemmed from more intrinsic motivation, such as for learning and self-actualization.

Taking advantage of a teachable moment to reinforce the value of safeguarding credibility:

A protégé had made it clear he adhered to a value set that he never played favorites when making decisions affecting the team; every member of the team was equally valuable and had a special role that he or she was assigned and trusted to fulfill. Yet, in one session, the protégé spoke of a staff member with whom he had had dinner in the past weekend, and whom he had asked to take a look at how other team members were performing (without the supervisory authority to perform this assessment), and provide him with some feedback. When the mentor heard this information, he raised the issue of the protégé's credibility in the eyes of others on the team, as it seemed he had given special and unique responsibilities to a staff member in a manner that contradicted his espoused value of equal treatment for all. The protégé admitted he had thought less about the credibility issue and more about the value of learning valuable information about team operations from an insider.

The teachable moment arose when the mentor ascertained a deviation from professed values, which can be highly detrimental to safeguarding professional credibility. Given the importance of maintaining a steadfast commitment to credibility-enhancing behaviors, the teachable moment is one with significant learning implications. Credibility is best addressed when circumstances test this credibility, not when the issues are less salient to discussions of how values align with behaviors.

Teachable moments clearly are those with an emotional component: euphoria about an achievement, yielding a discussion about the achievement's meaning; anxiety about the future, yielding a discussion of different strategies to mitigate future risks; sadness or shame about a circumstance, yielding a discussion about how to avoid the negative outcome going forward. Teachable moments are those that open the protégé up for insights or reinforcement of critical points the mentor has made in the past, but need further substantiation. Mentors can plan their learning interventions to coincide with a future teachable moment, and when that moment arrives, mentors should be ready to pounce on the opportunity to take advantage of the advantageous timing the teaching moment provides.

Whereas there is a spontaneous quality to identifying and leveraging a teaching moment that has emerged for a protégé, the thoughtful and prescient mentor will anticipate a potential teaching moment based on how circumstances are occurring and the way they relate to the protégé's development objectives.

Case example: A mentor and protégé identify public speaking and platform skills as an area for development. The protégé has received mixed reviews when speaking to groups or performing as a trainer, with some liking her style while others complain about her lack of connection to the audience. The protégé is anxious when speaking to groups, but she prepares well, by planning and rehearsing her presentations to ensure that the talk covers all the material the audience needs and expects.

The mentor has observed the protégé making these presentations, and has fed back to her occasionally that she might connect better to the audience if she almost turned the presentation into a conversation with the audience, a give-and-take rather than being fully beholden to a set of PowerPoint slides. The mentor suggests this might leave the audience feeling better about their training or learning experience with her as a presenter.

The mentor attends a presentation the protégé has prepared for and discussed in their mentoring sessions. The protégé is following a speaker who presents with great charisma and engaging style, without substantial notes or slides to prompt the content in the talk. The protégé's comparatively stiff delivery of her material seems to engender considerable boredom in the training group. Some attendees get up in the middle of the talk to make calls. In feedback forms on the presenters, the protégé receives relatively low marks on presentation style.

The mentor and protégé go for a drink at the hotel bar after her presentation. The protégé is in low spirits, and states she is increasingly convinced that her method and delivery just don't work well.

The mentor suggests, "How about if we do it my way next time: no notes, no slides, just like you were talking to me and asking me questions like you do. It can't end up any worse than what you just went through!" The protégé agrees, and in subsequent meetings, they roleplay platform speaking without notes and with a more conversational style.

The mentor in the case example might have another teachable moment later, if, after the protégé's next presentation in which the different delivery style was attempted, the audience responded very favorably. The teachable moment would be reinforcing an effective and career-enhancing behavior, and gaining a commitment to apply the same techniques in future platform speaking opportunities.

Summary

Teachable moments are those that offer a special and circumstances-driven window of opportunity to promote learning of a skill or set of knowledge. When planning their approach to advancing the learning of protégés, mentors should identify potential teachable moments that would reinforce the issues they wish to make that apply to skill development. Doing so transforms the Mentoring Plan into a dynamic approach to timing the delivery of important learning and development messages that the mentor wishes to emphasize.

CHAPTER 14

Powerful Practice #9 of Really Great Mentors:

Reinforce the Value of Lifelong Learning

Workplace research demonstrates that in the next decade, 75 percent of current workers will need significant retraining. Protégés are more likely than not to change jobs and careers many times in their lives—indeed, transitioning to new roles is the reason why mentoring is provided. For mentors, these facts translate into a need to emphasize that the learning process protégés are engaged in is just a beginning, not the end. The philosopher Immanuel Kant wrote that "It is a duty of man to himself to cultivate his natural powers (of the spirit, of the mind and of the body) as means to all kinds of possible ends. Man owes it to himself not to let his natural predispositions and capacities (which his reason can use someday) remain unused, and not to leave them, as it were, to rust." Effective mentors agree with this premise: keep learning or your skills will become quickly outdated and antiquated.

Mentors need to embrace, advocate for, and integrate the value of lifelong learning into performance of their support role. Protégés' knowledge of their profession and indeed of the world around them must always expand and adapt to their evolving learning needs. The knowledge required to assume higher professional roles expands and changes each day. Mentoring represents the value of continuing education, as considerable ongoing teaching occurs throughout the course of the mentor–protégé relationship. But this Powerful Practice of Really Great Mentors involves more than the learning that occurs as mentors and protégés interact. It advocates that mentors reinforce the value of developing healthy knowledge-enhancing habits that last a lifetime. Every day offers nearly unlimited opportunities to gain the type of knowledge that can be instrumental in the protégé's future.

It is essential to learn on a continuous basis if you want to remain relevant and credible. By continuing to learn new things and build on a prior knowledge base, you remains valuable—not only because of what you now know, but because of the potential to use that knowledge as a springboard for additional skill-building and learning later. Mentors need to convey the guiding principle that lifelong learning is a primary driver of an individual's ongoing value within an organization. Consequently, protégés have a responsibility to themselves to remain challenged to learn as much as they can about themselves and the skills needed along their nearly limitless professional learning curve.

A truism upon which this Powerful Practice is based is that knowledge about practically everything expands dynamically every day. This is truer today than ever before. Keeping up to date with emerging developments in the world, in one's industry, and in one's profession is a complex endeavor. Frankly, it is hard work, requiring substantial time and focus. When mentors place a high value on developing lifelong learning habits within protégés, they are facilitating a transition from receiving professional guidance from a mentor to more self-actuated continuing education.

Lifelong learning serves the following key functions:

※ **Validating up-to-date professional competency and credibility.** When protégés gain new knowledge about the work they do, they confirm that they are current about what it takes to bring value to the organization.

※ **Improving outcomes.** Ongoing skill-building translates into better products and services with which the protégé is involved.

※ **Improving judgment for key decision-making.** Added knowledge engenders the power to select between a set of alternatives, often in an environment of high complexity.

※ **Enhancing professional satisfaction and preventing burnout.** Learning is an exciting and fulfilling process, with positive impacts on protégés' motivation to fulfill their own potential.

What can the mentor do to enhance the prospect of lifelong learning by the protégé? Firstly, in the Mentoring Plan, mentors need to ensure that the protégé address knowledge gaps in the here-and-now. This requires a careful analysis of the protégé's current strengths and challenges, to identify more immediate training needs. But the plan also needs to be aligned with anticipated knowledge gaps in the future. This assessment requires a more complex analysis of trends that impact training in years to come. The mentoring process needs to consider the direction of the protégé's career and of the professional competencies that will be required at higher levels along the competence gradient.

The Mentoring Plans we discussed in Powerful Practice #7 should have a Lifelong Learning section, in which longer-term learning activities and objectives are identified. This section of the plan focuses on routine continuing education, particularly through self-study. Such self-study learning opportunities abound in today's Internet-mediated world. Google-enabled searches lead individuals to scholarly papers, blogs, articles, and a range of other content that can be very instructive. The Internet has communities of interest that enable those in the same profession to interact both in real time and asynchronously. Consequently, self-learning in contemporary culture does not necessarily require that the protégé take a trip to the library or attend a class or other organized learning event. It can be done in the evenings, at home, or in other offline timeframes. Mentors can conduct a parallel exploration of available learning opportunities or content on the Internet that could address the protégé's current and future knowledge gaps, and make recommendations to integrate into the Lifelong Learning section of the Mentoring Plan.

Of course, lifelong learning can also occur in more formalized educational contexts, with opportunities to get credit for participation in continuing education courses. These courses are offered routinely by universities, professional associations, private training companies, and specialized subject matter experts. Mentors apply their own experience about the best match of training opportunities and training programs that have proven effective in advancing a certain set of professional skills.

The following is an example of a Lifelong Learning section within a Mentoring Plan developed for and with a protégé:

Lifelong Learning

How the protégé will maintain an ongoing, self-directed effort to advance professional knowledge and skills throughout his or her professional life.

Activities	Method	Frequency	Desired Outcomes
Assemble and review content related to profession and/or industry	Perform Internet searches for content with keywords, download selected content for review	Weekly	Perform self study on selected topics to advance valuable knowledge
Attend Webinars on topics of interest	Identify sources of Webinar content and join meetings of interest	Monthly	Enhance understanding of best practices

Join groups on professionally oriented social media sites; participate in online discussions	Join a professional group on LinkedIn or specialized blog; review postings	Daily	Remain abreast of trends, ideas, developments
Read books on management, leadership, personal effectiveness training, or other topics of interest	Take trip to bookstore (brick and mortar or online) and purchase books on topics of interest. Read books in personal time (during travel, in evenings, etc.)	Monthly	Enhance understanding of best practices
Meet Continuing Education credit requirements for professional credential	Participate in sufficient CEU credit courses, online or in-person, to maintain professional credential	Ongoing	Retain credential when renewals are required

Mentors need to role-model this characteristic they are encouraging their protégés to embrace. Lifelong learning for mentors includes training in mentoring skills (discussed in the next chapter) and enhancing overall knowledge so that they can be a source of technical learning throughout the course of the relationship.

Summary

If it is a given that knowledge requirements will change and evolve throughout a professional lifetime, then it is also a given that professionals need to maintain healthy habits related to augmenting professional knowledge throughout one's lifetime. Mentors can guide this process. They recommend sources of valuable information to return to, again and again, such as blogs or writings of a particularly valuable subject matter expert. Mentors model this behavior as well. By demonstrating the value to themselves of maintaining an interest in lifelong learning, mentors build their credibility in this role and develop ideas for future learning opportunities of which protégés can take advantage.

End of
The ❾ Powerful Practices
of Really Great Mentors

CHAPTER 15

Approaches to Mentor Training

The concept upon which mentoring is based—that there is value in learning skills from those with more experience than you—pertains to mentor training as well. Prospective mentors who do not embrace their need for training are unlikely to be truly committed to or effective while performing in the mentoring role. How can you advocate for lifelong learning, Powerful Practice #9, if you don't see its benefit for yourself? Mentoring is enacted within a framework that places substantial value on continuous learning and growth. It is quite natural and role-congruent, then, for mentors to seek training on their own, to ensure that the time they spend in this role is as effective as possible.

We train mentors by applying a learning model that builds upon itself, logically and incrementally. We recommend that new mentors participate in the full range of training we describe in the following paragraphs, at least once. Then, the mentor can self-identify a need for additional training within a certain module, based on issues and skill-development needs experienced once actual mentoring begins.

Basic Training—Mentoring "Boot Camp"

We begin a course of instruction for mentors by establishing an instructional environment to reinforce the basic skills that were discussed in Chapter 2: the dynamics of self-actualization and human motivation, empathy, self-awareness, and active listening. Some say that you either have these understanding or "people skills" or you don't, so such training might be wasteful. We disagree—our experience is that they can be learned, or applied with greater discipline once training has reinforced their value. Time and again, we have seen leaders return to the emotionally intelligent behaviors they learned in workshops and coaching we have led for them, because they have developed a sincere appreciation for how valuable they are. Armed with an understanding of how to express greater empathy and responsiveness to others' needs, they practice the skills that support self-awareness an empathy continuously.

Prior to receiving such training, mentors might respond to certain workplace stimuli as they always have. These responses have often been engrained for years. They might involve frustration with the shortcomings of others, resignation about the futility of helping someone, or of considering one's own perspectives before trying to understand others' perspectives. But the mentor who goes through the Boot Camp training becomes more self-aware, and works through such "me-oriented" responses. They have learned that it is the "other-oriented" responses that engender the results they seek.

Certainly, some leaders/mentors have well-developed interpersonal skills already. The truth is that the higher one rises in an organizational hierarchy—where most senior mentors can be found—the more likely it is that one possesses the emotional and social intelligence to succeed in demanding roles. The prior achievements of effective mentors foretell some level of emotional and social intelligence. For these prospective mentors, instruction in the core skills can be considered "refresher training."

We have found that those with strong people skills actually enjoy this training a great deal. It reminds them of the attributes that have become part of their leadership style. It also increases their awareness of instances when others around them do not demonstrate self-awareness, empathy, or an ability to listen. This assessment helps them respond with empathy rather than frustration to such individuals. When mentors have well-developed interpersonal skills, they understand that these are the skills they need to role-model to protégés, as much as the more technical skills of a professional role.

Mentoring Boot Camp training begins with an overview of emotional intelligence (EQ). We define it and offer real-life examples of its value in one's career. Trainees are solicited to share their personal experiences applying or being on the receiving end of sound emotional intelligence skills. Of course, experiences of poor EQ typically are raised as well. These experiences invariably demonstrate the negative career impact of demonstrating poor self-awareness, self-regulation, empathy, and relationship management skills.

The Boot Camp sets up roleplaying simulations of circumstances requiring the practicing of empathy. Listening skills and methods to enhance situational understanding are reviewed and exercised. For example, we might ask trainees to pair up and share with their role-playing mentor an actual development need they are experiencing or have experienced. The exercise has the dual value of promoting self-awareness in the trainee roleplaying the protégé, and promoting the empathic listening methods we advocate that mentors integrate into their mentoring practice so that it becomes almost second nature to them.

We also review some basic theories of behavior science at work, such as Maslow's Hierarchy of Needs model. The concepts of self-actualization and what self-actualizing behaviors really look like are reviewed. Mentor trainees are prompted to discuss what self-actualization means for them, how mentoring contributes to this process, and how mentoring can best facilitate a sense of personal and career fulfillment in protégés.

Next-Level Training—The Mentoring Role and Its Requirements

The next phase of mentor training supports mentors' understanding of their role and objectives in performing this role. Trainees are provided with a definitional construct of mentoring that impacts how they should view their role and the objectives of performing in the mentoring role. The training reviews the components of psychosocial mentoring and career coaching, noting their differences but also how a blending of these two types of mentoring approaches tends to work best. The training is presented typically in a lecture and discussion format, with prospective mentors asked to discuss how the true definition of mentoring might differ from their perceptions of the role prior to training. It is important to encourage mentors to embrace all aspects of the mentoring role, especially for those who might view the role as one that places a heavy emphasis on reviewing "here is how I do it" skill instruction. Training emphasizes that the mentoring relationship is far more complex and often far more intense than one focused on simple instructional content.

Final Training Phase—Overview of the 9 Powerful Practices of Really Great Mentors Model

Once mentors have a solid grasp of what their mentoring activities can achieve, we begin our review of the 9 Powerful Practices of Really Great Mentors we have shared in this book. The training blends instruction/discussion and roleplaying, to reinforce the value of each of these mentoring practices. In some instances during this training, mentors are placed in groups and asked to produce a product that relates to a Powerful Practice.

For example, groups may be asked to develop a set of stretch goals for hypothetical protégés. The discussion within the groups will raise the risks and vulnerabilities we discussed in Chapter 9, on identifying stretch goals, and find a common comfort level with the most appropriate stretch goal. Some groups may truly reach for the stars, while others will prefer to set goals that involve a "reach" from current circumstances, but appear to most to be attainable with reasonable progress, motivation, and focused effort by the protégé.

We discuss role-modeling behaviors, intrinsic versus extrinsic motivation, people styles and their impact on mentoring, and the concept of enhancing personal and professional credibility. In a different session, the training reviews strategic-thinking skills, developing a Mentoring Plan with protégé input, identifying teachable moments, and advocating the importance of lifelong learning.

Apropos to the merits of lifelong learning, we present the notion that mentors benefit from refresher training throughout the period of time they perform in the mentoring role, and inform them how they can take advantage of refresher training opportunities. Often, we can deliver such follow-up training via group Webinars and virtual training sessions, which mentors can easily fit into their busy work week. These follow-up refresher training offerings are, in essence, "mentor the mentor"-focused skill-development learning. Active mentors support each other and share experiences that demonstrate how the role can be delivered most effectively, all in the context of the information provided in the three-part Mentor Training program.

Afterword

Mentoring is a highly dynamic role, focused on the learning needs of individual protégés. Our model is intended to enhance the dynamism of the relationship, both as a means to achieve better results and to engender greater satisfaction among mentors in performing this role. We and the seasoned mentors we interviewed for this book have found that the more exciting and satisfying the mentoring process is for the mentor, the more the protégé is likely to gain from the relationship.

The 9 practices we present in our model are not sequential or iterative. You no doubt have noticed this already, given the many times we have cross-referenced another Powerful Practice when addressing one in particular. The 9 practices interface extensively with each other, and blend together to form a fully integrated approach to the mentoring role.

Each practice has its own correct time or place for applying it. Consequently, it is up to you to select when and where to use the model's recommended mentoring methods, alone or in combination with each other. Mentoring involves not just having strong intuitive instincts about the learning needs of others, but also having the awareness of messages your intuition sends you. Intuitive awareness will engender the most targeted responses. Mentoring is an instructional art, built upon developing a keen sense of what students require, when they require it, how they will best receive or absorb instruction, and the outcomes that demonstrate that the instruction "took." Mentors gain an intuitive sense of the best practice to use, at the right time and place.

Always remember that a mentor is part advisor, part sponsor, part role model, part teacher, part counselor, part friend, part coach. Actually, the list goes on much further than this. Each practice we have advanced ties in to one or more of these roles. The best mentors are those who can perform all of these roles competently, concurrently, and confidently.

The type of mentoring we have discussed in this book involves a 1:1 type of mentoring. Actually, several other forms of mentoring exist. For example, considerable attention has been dedicated to the concept of Peer Mentoring, a process through which an individual with a specific experience (peer mentor) advises a person who is new to that experience (the peer mentee). An example would be an experienced worker being a peer mentor to a new company hire, the peer mentee, in a particular occupation or workplace. Clearly, this is not the type of mentoring we have discussed. At former jobs we held in our careers, we called it "the buddy system." But it could have value at a senior level, for enhancing "mentor the mentor"-type training. A system would be valuable to have in place in which experienced mentors share their experiences and advice to other mentors in an organization.

Another type of mentoring delivered in the workplace is called "Reverse Mentoring." In this type of mentoring, the competence gradient focuses on a skill the protégé has that the mentor does not—the opposite of the typical mentor–protégé experience paradigm. Those in a protégé role actually mentor those in a mentor role. An example might be tied to use of technology or social media. A younger professional, who grew up using computers, apps, and mobile devices as an integral component not just to their studies but also to living their lives, may offer guidance on how to leverage such technology for a mentor who grew up in a paper-and-pencil, non-computerized world.

This type of mentoring can occur in an existing mentor–protégé relationship. The mentor might have the self-awareness to say to his or her protégé, "Okay, it's time for you to mentor me. You know far more about downloading the right apps to perform a certain function. Teach me how it's done." The reverse mentoring does not get into psychosocial types of mentoring typically—it remains in the instructional or technical coaching sphere. But it can add potency to the relationship, reflecting the opportunity the relationship provides for a truly two-way, mutual learning dichotomy.

Group Mentoring is another type of mentoring support. It is typically performed by a single mentor, but the protégé or mentee is a team or group. An example of this type of mentoring might be a CEO Emeritus or Professor Emeritus mentoring the active executive group of his former company, or, in the case of the Professor Emeritus, the current faculty chairs as a group. The focus is on the group or team's capability to function well together, within an interdependent set of different executive functions. The skills being mentored are team-building, team effectiveness, and enhancing group synergies toward common objectives. Mentors of this type have a more holistic perspective of the mentee client for which they are providing guidance. They have been through the processes of collaborating within an executive group, and understand the processes that work best and the pitfalls to effective work coordination.

There actually may be times when such a mentor might get involved in a more 1:1 mentoring process with an individual whom the mentor has identified for "extra help." Such extra support need not be due to failings of the group-turned-individual protégé, but might be due to an extraordinary upside potential seen in him or her. But in the end, this type of mentoring is focused on positive outcomes for the group or team as a whole.

Mentoring in any of its forms is certainly a worthy calling. It affirms a life dedicated, at least in part, to the enrichment of others. It is an apt culmination of a professional life within which one has gained experience and achieved steadily advancing domain knowledge. Mentoring is an activity cultivated by an interest in sharing this experience and knowledge with others. We all have heard the saying about the extent to which one should spend one's wealth in later years: "You can't take it with you." The same can be said for one's wisdom and accumulated experience. Sharing it produces its own rewards, not the least of which is the admiration and appreciation one receives from protégés and all of those close to them, for the willingness of the mentor to "pay it forward" on their behalf.

We hope this information has been valuable for you as you begin or continue your mentoring role. We have opened a Facebook site for *9 Powerful Practices of Really Great Mentors* where you can follow us and post impressions that you have of the book and its contents (*www.facebook.com/9PracticesofReal lyGreatMentors*). We've been mentored effectively about how to use social media to gain connections to our readers! Let us know how these practices work for you in real life.

We'll see you there!

———

Common Questions Asked About Performing in the Mentoring Role

Q: Can anyone be a mentor? Why or why not?

A: Mentoring is not for everyone—at least not mentoring in its fullest definition. Fulfilling this role depends not just on the level of skills and experience one has gained that could be of value to a prospective protégé, but also on one's orientation toward supporting others. Mentors are those who can focus on the needs of others and craft guidance and instruction that matches the mentees' needs. Individuals who do not have such an "other-orientation" or who do not see the value of lifelong learning are probably not suited for the mentoring role. We will say, however, that most individuals have "the mentor within." It just needs an opportunity to come out, for the well-matched mentee, with suitable training.

Q: How do I go about finding someone to mentor?

A: Many professional associations sponsor mentoring programs. In some cases you can volunteer yourself as a mentor, then complete an application and profile, much like one we described in this book. At your own workplace, a mentoring program may be in place or may be under consideration. Talk to your human capital people about the prospect of participating in such a program.

Q: What are some common pitfalls that people experience in the mentor–protégé relationship?

A: The most common pitfalls occur in formal mentoring programs, in which matches are made more arbitrarily or without a more natural relationship-building process. There is no guarantee that two people, a more senior person and a more junior person, are well-matched to work together in a mentor–protégé relationship. The best antidote for this pitfall is to provide opportunities for the protégé to select a mentor, and follow this selection with opportunities for the protégé to meet the mentor before the relationship is cemented or made formal. This gives the pair an opportunity to perceive if the relationship has an opportunity to work out well, or not.

Q: How can the mentor best deal with his or her own personal biases and blind spots? (Everyone has them!)

A: Mentors need a firm grounding in the skills that comprise emotional intelligence, one of which is appreciating the value of self-awareness and trying to build self-awareness on a continuous basis. The best mentors are those who seek feedback, look to expand their own self-awareness, and have a support system of their own around them to help them address any instances when feedback does not match their own perceptions about skills and challenges.

Mentors can also participate in a "360-Degree Multi-rater Feedback Survey Process." In this process, a mentor chooses a superior, peers, subordinates, and any others with familiarity about the mentor's competencies and challenges, to take a survey. In the survey, raters provide feedback on different measures of personal and professional effectiveness. When honestly and openly provided, such feedback can go a long way to addressing one's blind spots.

Q: Is it really possible to "learn" EQ? Is it really that important?

A: Gaining a higher EQ is vital to the ability to role-model emotionally intelligent behaviors for protégés. The best outcomes of mentoring occur when the mentor has credibility and earns the confidence of the protégé. Applying emotionally intelligent behaviors to a range of circumstances—being resilient and optimistic, practicing empathy, managing conflict, and so on—builds trust in the mentor–protégé relationship.

We believe EQ can be learned, or certainly improved. Take a course in emotional intelligence, sooner rather than later, if you haven't already.

Q: Must mentoring always take place in person?

A: No. Often a long-term mentor–protégé relationship moves to more virtual means of communication due to relocations, life changes, and so on. Today's technologies, such as Skype, enables video-based interactions, allowing both parties to interact synchronously and with the ability to see behavioral cues, and enables the mentor and protégé to maintain their relationship quite well. Clearly, the in-person method is ideal, but not completely necessary.

Bibliography

Bolton, Robert, and Dorothy Grover Bolton. *People Styles at Work*. New York: AMACOM, 1996.

Covey, Stephen R. *The 7 Habits of Highly Effective People*. Fireside, New York, 1989.

Deci, Edward L., and Richard M. Ryan. "Motivation and Education: The Self-Determination Perspective." *Educational Psychologist* 26, no. 3 & 4 (1991): 325–346.

Goleman, Daniel. *Emotional Intelligence*. New York: Bantam Books, 1995.

———. *Working With Emotional Intelligence*. New York: Bantam Books, 1998.

Havighurst, Robert James. *Human Development and Education*. Ann Arbor, Mich.: Longmans, Green, 1953.

Kagans, Belle Rose, and John L. Cotton. "Mentor Functions and Outcomes: A Comparison of Men and Women in Formal and Informal Mentoring Relationships." *Journal of Applied Psychology* 84, no. 4 (1999): 529–550.

Kagans, Belle Rose, and Kathy E. Kram. *The Handbook of Mentoring at Work.* Thousand Oaks, Calif.: Sage Publications, 2007.

Kagans, Belle Rose, John L. Cotton, and Janice S. Miller. "Marginal Mentoring: The Effects of Type of Mentor, Quality of Relationship, and Program Design on Work and Career Attitudes." *Academy of Management Journal* 43, no. 6 (2000): 1177–1194.

Kohn, Stephen E., and Vincent D. O'Connell. *9 Powerful Practices of Really Great Bosses.* Franklin Lakes, N.J.: Career Press, 2005.

Markovitz, Daniel. "The Folly of Stretch Goals." *Harvard Business Review* (April 20, 2012). *https://hbr.org/2012/04/the-folly-of-stretch-goals.*

Mariani, Bette. "The Effect of Mentoring on Career Satisfaction of Registered Nurses and Intent to Stay in the Nursing Profession." *Nursing Research and Practice* 2012 (2012): Epub Article ID 168278, 9 pages.

Megginson, David, and David Clutterbuck. *Techniques for Coaching and Mentoring.* London: Elsevier Butterworth Heinemann, 2005.

O'Connell, Vincent. "SOLID Account Management: White Paper #1—Core Principles of Client Relationship Management," available at *www.workandpeople.com* (2008).

Ryan, Richard M., and Edward L. Deci. "Self-Determination Theory and the Facilitation of Intrinsic Motivation, Social Development, and Well-Being." *American Psychologist* 55, no. 1 (January 2000): 68–78.

Sheldon, Kennon M., Richard M. Ryan, Laird J. Rawsthorne, and Barbara Ilardi. "Trait Self and True Self: Cross-Role Variation in the Big-Five Personality Traits and Its Relations With Psychological Authenticity and Subjective Well-Being." *Journal of Personality and Social Psychology* 73, no. 6 (1997): 1380–1393.

Whitmore, John. *Coaching for Performance: Growing People, Performance and Purpose, 3rd Ed.* London: Nicholas Brealey, 2002.

Wiltshire, Susan Ford. *Athena's Disguises: Mentors in Everyday Life.* Louisville, Ky.: Westminster John Knox Press, 1998.

Index

215

About the Authors

Mr. Stephen Kohn is president of Work & People Solutions, a human resources management, leadership development, and executive coaching firm based in White Plains, New York. He is the coauthor with Vincent O'Connell of five books on people management and teamwork, and he has appeared as a guest commentator on topics relating to organizational leadership for numerous media, including WCBS radio in New York and *Newsday* in Long Island, N.Y. He graduated from Cornell University and completed his graduate studies at Adelphi University. Mr. Kohn is also an adjunct professor of management at Long Island University, teaching MBA courses dedicated to work, people, and productivity.

Mr. Vincent O'Connell is president of B-SOLID Coaching and Training, a training and consulting firm focused on improving the people management skills of organizational leaders, based in McLean, Virginia. Mr. O'Connell served in executive positions in marketing at various hospitals, and he was a consultant for the Hay Group and Buck Consultants. A graduate of Brown University, Mr. O'Connell did his graduate work in Human Resources Management at Cornell University. He has authored numerous articles for professional journals, and coauthored five books with Mr. Kohn.